Earth, Wind & Wildlife

Earth, Wind & Wildlife

THE CHALLENGES OF COTTAGE GARDENING

Lillian Newbery and Gordon Handley

The BOSTON MILLS PRESS

Published in 1997 by
Boston Mills Press
132 Main Street
Erin, Ontario
N0B 1T0
Tel 519-833-2407
Fax 519-833-2195
www.boston-mills.on.ca

Distributed in Canada by
General Distribution Services Inc.
30 Lesmill Road
Toronto, Canada M3B 2T6
Tel 416-445-3333
Fax 416-445-5967
e-mail customer.service@ccmailgw.genpub.com

Distributed in the United States by
General Distribution Services Inc.
85 River Rock Drive, Suite 202
Buffalo, New York 14207
Toll-free 1-800-805-1083
Fax 416-445-5967
e-mail customer.service@ccmailgw.genpub.com

01 00 99 98 97   1 2 3 4 5

Cataloging in Publication Data

Newbery, Lillian, 1945–
Earth, wind and wildlife: the challenges of cottage gardening
Includes bibliographical references.
ISBN 1-55046-205-9

1. Gardening - Ontario, Northern.   2. Gardens - Ontario,
Northern. I. Handley, Gordon.   II. Title
SB451.36.C3N48 1997   635'.09713'1   97-930709-0

Design by Gillian Stead
Printed in Hong Kong,
by Book Art Inc., Toronto

Contents

AT LEFT: *Lilies and more than sixty different perennials attract bees to a hillside garden. Closer to the lake tall plants are staked.*

Gardeners don't spend much time in hammocks.
A family toiled for years at their cottage baring the magnificent rock — and planting to enhance it.

Introduction

Gardeners in Muskoka, Haliburton, Parry Sound, Georgian Bay and the Kawarthas face plenty of challenges.

Deer nibble on ground covers. Chipmunks devour an entire crop of peas in one night. Winds dry the soil, often sparse to begin with. Rocks poke up everywhere. As several gardeners wryly noted, "We all have rock gardens." Away from the water, frosts linger into June and strike again in late August. And for those cottagers who are "up north" only at weekends or perhaps for a month, it's a short season for working in and enjoying a garden.

As for the weather, every year it is pronounced exceptional — the coldest in years, the hottest in memory, so cloudy that summer didn't ever seem to get started, or, particularly irritating to gardeners, cursed with swarms of mosquitoes and black-flies in quantities no one can recall occurring before.

This book is intended to share the experiences of successful gardeners in the southern edge of the Precambrian Shield, what some people call cottage country.

Some of these gardens belong to full-time residents who moved to their beloved out-of-town property to experience the seasons year-in, year-out. Most of the gardens visited in this book, however, were created by cottagers during vacations. It's amazing that anyone manages to garden in addition to traditional cottage pursuits such as family picnics, boating, supervising children swimming, entertaining, summer theatre, reading and the inevitable cottage maintenance. For some enthusiasts, retirement provides the long-awaited opportunity to concentrate on gardening. Each of the gardens in this book has its own distinctive style, reflecting not only the individual gardener's tastes and experience, but also the particular challenges and possibilities inherent in the properties themselves.

For some, the glory of a lakeside cottage is characterized by boathouse window boxes cascading with annuals. Other families work for generations plotting perennial gardens laid out between classic granite walkways. One gardener specializes in ferns, another recently started a scree garden, one experiments with mosses, several tend lily ponds, and one has been cultivating vegetables on an island for a quarter of a century.

While seasonal and full-time residents seem equally passionate about pursuing exotic seed strains and unusual perennials, some seek out native plants, now stocked by a number of nurseries in Muskoka, and strive to conserve the indigenous species already growing on their properties.

Gardeners may labour on their own, learning as they go, or exchange tips and transplants with green-thumb neighbours. Others share information through thriving horticultural societies. A vision of "what might be" animates most cottage gardeners, who dwell in what Barry Broadfoot called his book about Western Canada, "Tomorrow Country."

Even when they knew to the tips of their fingers that the plants were not at their peak, the gardeners generously shared their secluded spaces, affording readers an open tour of gardens that are, with one exception, personal and private.

Strawberries spread along the point of this exposed outer island in Georgian Bay off Pointe-au-Baril.

Lilies thrive in gardens at many cottages.

The one public garden in the book recreates what might have been planted by First Nations people and Jesuit missionaries at Sainte-Marie Among the Hurons in the 1600s. It's a reminder of a time when a group's survival depended in part on its knowledge of agriculture.

If a theme emerges from conversations with these gardeners, it's a trend toward working with the environment. Part of the fun for gardeners is learning what works and what doesn't at their cottages. As naturalist and author R. D. Lawrence put it, anyone expecting to come to the country and reproduce the garden enjoyed in the city is doomed to failure.

It has been by suggested by others that any interference with the indigenous landscape results in an undesirable footprint. This does not appear to be a widely held view at this point, but certainly, as the twentieth century draws to a close,

it's no longer considered eccentric to think twice about disturbing the natural flora and rocks of the shoreline, to encourage wildflowers and grasses, and to forego the use of fertilizers near waterways. Sensitivity to location and integrating a garden with its surroundings have always been at the core of good gardening.

My hope for the reader is that you find both inspiration and practical tips within these pages to help you meet the challenges of cottage gardening. Particular gardens may suggest a result you would like to achieve or confirm an impression of what you do not want. Alternatively, if you prefer reading to gardening, savour your visit to these gardens, the way they were one summer. As Mirabel Osler notes in *A Gentle Plea for Chaos*, at no moment will a garden stay immobile; it is always becoming something else.

Hundreds of narcissi bulbs buried for decades under rocks, separated and replanted, welcome spring.

CHAPTER 1

Rocks

For more than twenty centuries, natural stones have played a prominent and symbolic role in Chinese gardens. The Japanese developed the use of uncut stones into a gardening art. In the Western tradition, however, the ideal of creating a garden of paradise meant keeping the wild at bay. The wilderness was excluded by cut stones walling in the garden space. Order was imposed on the landscape by terraces, paths, steps and planting beds called parterres.

By the eighteenth century, a romantic mood softened the geometric designs and embraced grottoes and rockeries composed of natural rather than cut stone. In the 1860s, when European collectors began cultivating alpines and rock plants, they tried to replicate the environments of these high-country plants with gravel-strewn slopes called scree, and rocky meadows and rocky outcrops.

Now, at the end of the twentieth century, a new appreciation of the environment has led to an interest in natural gardens, conferring importance on the use of stone in its natural form.

For gardeners on the Precambrian Shield, natural rock occurs as an unavoidable ingredient in the garden. The Canadian Shield covers 1,771,000 square miles (4,533,760 km²), stretching almost without interruption over two-thirds of Eastern Canada.

Cottagers and year-round residents in this area exploit the rocks at hand as part of garden design. Rock crevices can serve as natural plant containers, and do, particularly on islands in Georgian Bay. While some cottagers may buy cut stone to construct a path to the lake, most of their gardens are characterized by the use of natural rocks, churned up millions of years ago by retreating glaciers. Rocks are heaved from place to place by enterprising gardeners to form retaining walls, windbreaks, stepping stones, and edging for flower beds.

For moving rocks, any aids to spare the back are recommended, particularly wheelbarrows, crowbars and ramps. For lifting, a squatting position using the thigh muscles is best.

In making paths, stepping stones should be at least 14 inches (35 cm) long for stability, and if they are to be bordered by plants, extra width should be allowed in the expectation that plants will spill over onto the path. To start, walk the proposed path and mark your footfalls. For a base, lay several inches of crushed rock and a couple of inches of sand over tamped earth. Lay stones at their widest dimension horizontally and set them 4 to 5 inches (about 11 cm) apart, in clusters rather than vertical lines. Paths should be widened at the beginning and end and at curves. Steps should be as wide as paths and pitched slightly forward for quick drainage. It is considerate to provide landings.

Paths at cottages and in the country differ from paths in city gardens, suggests Henry Koch, horticultural interpreter at the University of Guelph Arboretum. In the city, the garden path traditionally take walkers to "view" borders and beds. At a cottage, a path through the garden takes us on a journey and provides an entry into the landscape to explore nature — an entry into what has changed, what is in bloom, what insects are visiting, what is going on around the bend.

Changes in bedrock, by contrast, are measured in the tens of thousands of years. In its endurance and solid, sombre beauty, the exposed rock defines the landscape. Existing rocks and rock formations can be exploited with great success by cottage gardeners, and sometimes even moved for that purpose.

❧ DRAWN TO THE ROCKS ❧

From the lake, the eye sweeps up sloping bare rock to a rock patio framed by carpets of sedums and mosses — a perfect place for watching sunsets. To the right, timber-backed steps lined with pine needles lead through huckleberry bushes and a border shiny with periwinkle. In the lawn above, a waist-high boulder accents a semi-circular garden under a birch. Two rock gardens, one in sun, one in shade, frame steps to a wooden deck that runs along the front of the cottage.

The effect is so natural and harmonious you would never suspect the owners spent their first dozen summers here hauling, removing, uncovering, rolling, carrying and placing rocks. They turned to planting only about fifteen years ago and insist they are not serious gardeners.

An artist's eye informs the landscape. Ann and Don Campbell's son, David, teaches fine art and is the chief designer of the garden. Their daughter Deane adds her refining touch to the borders and pathways. Ann is actually more drawn to the shape and surface of rocks than to plants and Don is involved in all aspects of the landscaping. From the first, Don recalls, they sought a natural look.

When the family acquired the property on Lake Muskoka, the shoreline was covered with huge boulders. They had them removed by barge. On the east side, a swamp choked with jewelweed and oak stumps and dense with vegetation was

The cottagers at this site now prefer native and naturalized plants to cultivars. No pesticides or herbicides are used.

drained. Today it is carpeted with ground covers and plants such as Jacob's ladder, now seeding itself freely, and lady's mantle, which does well in the wet. Much of the rock now bare had been hidden in wild grasses matted in thin soil. They pulled this off by hand over four years, even building a special rickshaw-like cart to carry away the soil over uneven ground.

At one time a wooden patio sat up from the shore. David probed with a metal bar and found reasonably flat rock beneath. It was at this spot about eight years ago that the family constructed a rock patio, reached by stone stairs and backed by a rock wall. The weight and location of the rocks meant the work had to be carried out by hand, using handmade hoists, tripods and levers. Gardens were planted on either side using mother-of-thyme, sedums and mosses.

To make the unique pine-needle steps, the Campbells brought a trailer of sawdust, obtained free from a sawmill, for the base. They raked up new-fallen pine needles, and to keep them crisp and retain the red colour, stored them over winter in baskets in the garage. Then they laid the pine needles over the sawdust. The process keeps the steps weed-free for years and the pine needles can be replaced as they age.

For the rock gardens, the Campbells started by bringing plants from the city, but today favour plants native to the woodland or naturalized in Ontario. They

*Below a Lake Muskoka cottage, pine-needle steps descend through
a meticulously composed rockscape of ground covers and huckleberry bushes.*

are constantly experimenting with new plants. Recently they tried purple, blue and pink morning glories, trained on string against the cottage wall. With about half a day of sun, they add colour and a vertical element to the landscape.

Shrubs — a ninebark, golden spirea, golden mock orange and white deutzia a form the background for the shady rock garden. Ferns, Golden Sceptre hosta, fringed bleeding heart, coral bells, sweet woodruff, pink mallow, sweet rocket, dwarf iris, oregano, coreopsis, pincushion spurge and mother-of-thyme provide foliage as attractive as the blooms. In the sunnier rock garden, phlox, astilbe, meadow rue, garlic chives, coleus, foxglove, Jacob's ladder and angelica flourish.

The Campbells find animals a destructive force in the garden. A groundhog devours hosta. A large herd of deer carves topiary trees out of an evergreen hedge, nibbles the buds of young plants and chews the phlox. One year the deer pulled out most of the periwinkle by the roots; now it's protected in winter with a staked plastic mesh.

At first the Campbells used topsoil in the garden, then moved to a triple-mix prepared soil. They compost leaves for mulch to enrich the soil, keep moisture in and reduce weeds. They use no pesticides or herbicides. David says they try to raise vigorous plants to discourage insects and that native plants appear more resistant to pests and disease.

The Campbells find woodland plants such as cohosh more fitting than the peony they brought from home. On the north-facing side of the cottage, in deep shade under the eaves, cohosh transplanted from the woods just behind forms lush mounds, contrasting with bright-coloured impatiens.

Some years ago, Ann noticed a plant with a leaf like a lily of the valley in a boggy spot just below the periwinkle bed. It was indeed a member of the lily family, *Clintonia borealis*, or bluebead lily. Transplanted to a place of honour at a front corner of the cottage, it spread into a pleasing cluster with yellow bell-shaped flowers followed by striking blue fruit. Visitors always ask what it is. And so a woodland plant that could easily be overlooked has become a star in this amazing Muskoka garden.

🌿 Unearthing a Hidden Garden 🌿

Neither Ron Jean-Marie nor his wife, Carolyn Moore, will never forget the day they discovered the hidden rock garden.

For several years, on weekends and holidays, they had been sprucing up the yard around a vacant Muskoka farmhouse. Built by Ron's great-grandfather in 1882 off the Juddhaven Road east of Minett, it was owned by an uncle who lived away. A tangle of grapevines, ash trees and scrub brush covered the front yard.

Ron had grown up nearby on Lake Rosseau and still owned a maple sugar bush next to the farmhouse. On breaks from their city jobs, Ron and Carolyn camped in a trailer in an open area in the sugar bush. They began clearing the overgrowth in front of the house, Ron hacking at the vines and digging out trees while Carolyn pulled weeds and cultivated the soil.

Their first find amazed them; it was a ring of some forty quartz rocks that his grandmother had collected to edge a garden. To celebrate, Carolyn planted petunias in the ring.

The next spring, phlox seeds that had lain dormant for decades began to sprout. The following year, the spires of wondrous rosy foxgloves shot up. Photos dating to the 1920s show foxgloves in a garden in the same location; a botanist friend has told them their foxgloves are of a form that isn't cultivated today.

Foxglove seeds lay dormant for years, germinating after the new owners cleared overgrowth, reawakening a hidden rock garden.

After "a lot of time, hard work and tears," the couple unearthed a bed of daffodil and narcissus bulbs below a rock outcrop. Under some rocks, as many as 100 bulbs were jammed into a cubic foot of soil. They separated more than 1,000 bulbs and replanted them in front of the house and in the sugar bush. Now, with the addition of some King Alfred daffodil bulbs, every spring about 2,500 narcissi burst into bloom, and crocuses, lily of the valley and vinca edge the trail to the bush.

Meanwhile, moving rocks and pulling out scrub trees, "we just kept moving west," Ron says. One day he called Carolyn over to where he was working. He had uncovered a set of stone steps west of the farmhouse, leading to the outline of a sunken rock garden. "You could see the form of the rocks, the shape, the way they were set out."

"He was so excited," Carolyn recalls. "We couldn't wait to get his mother here to see if she remembered the garden." Stone pathways between boulders led to several rock-ringed flower beds. Completely hidden, the garden had been reclaimed by the forest after his grandmother became too infirm to work outdoors in the late 1940s.

The rocks are so large it would have taken a team of horses to haul them to the site, Ron says. To reestablish the garden, they dug around and raised buried rocks and stones. "We like the rocks as much as the flowers," says Carolyn.

As they work the beds, they add a ready supply of composted soil from a shaded garden and cow manure from a neighbouring farm. They also fertilize with manure tea, sliding manure into an old birdseed sack, swishing it around in a pail of water and leaving it for a week or so. They take the tea to the flowers in a watering can. "It's cheap and it works great," says Ron.

So far, there's no running water in the house, but the garden has running water, thanks to a pump that Ron puts down by the well.

Plants that Ron's grandmother nurtured keep reappearing. "We found one little piece of purple phlox and moved it," reports Carolyn. "From that one little sprig that survived there are now forty to sixty plants." Her daisies and black-eyed Susans began growing again, as did her purple iris, hosta, bleeding heart and lilies. The foxgloves pop up in shades from pink to dark red. Gloriosa daisies, lilies, pinks, anchusa, yarrow and sedums have been added.

Jean Marie and Moore constructed a little frog pond, edged with snow-in-summer, orange lilies, foxglove and perennial geraniums. A cast-iron gnome with a red cap presides. Spiderwort, bugleweed, astilbe, columbine and dead nettle (*Lamium maculatum*), a small plant with hooded purple flowers, grow with tuberous begonias, cosmos and impatiens in the old sunken garden.

Eventually the couple purchased the farmhouse, known as the Homestead, and the adjoining 200 acres (80 ha). In 1995, Ron retired there, and Carolyn retired the next year. They joke that they're using the proceeds from one hobby, maple syrup production, to pay for the other hobby, gardening. And, of course, there's the income from the horseshoe pitch. Ron says "young pups" from the neighbourhood occasionally come over to challenge him and they might risk a dollar on a game.

"We're still uncovering beds and making new ones in front of the house," says Carolyn. Further flower beds are waiting to be discovered, they believe, to the side of the lawn below the house. The couple have transplanted peonies that

Manure tea poured from a watering can
fertilizes plants in the rediscovered rock garden.

had been shaded by trees. Elsewhere, they're moving wild roses from shade to light. "It's like a disease, you just keep going," adds Ron.

Hiking through the bush behind the house, Ron found an open pasture where, he recalled, a vegetable garden had been started by his great-grandfather. Today on the same site, in a patch about 120 by 60 feet (36 by 18 m), he and his wife grow an array of vegetables. They're also cultivating fruits and berries: muskmelon, plums, high-bush blueberries, gooseberries — "great jelly" — and Saskatoon berries. They plan to install an electric fence here to repel animals such as the persistent raccoon that demolished a giant pumpkin.

There are no problems with deer on the property, but a bear has destroyed seven bird feeders. "We're not only gardening wackos, we're bird wackos," says Ron. In August, says Carolyn's daughter, Shannon, it's actually dangerous to sit on the verandah, when as many as twenty hummingbirds will fight over the feeders. If you watch from a distance, they put on a tremendous show.

For the sign identifying the Homestead at the end of the driveway, Ron Jean-Marie and Carolyn Moore chose two significant symbols from their garden — hummingbirds and foxglove.

❦ ROCKERIES ON LAKE JOSEPH ❦

Granite paths, wide rock stairs and massive retaining walls suggest stability, order and permanence at a long-established garden on Lake Joseph.

In the early 1950s, the owners removed trees to open their sloped south shore to the sun and began work with a landscaper setting in the expansive rockwork that has defined the gardens since.

Frances Reid says that while the rockeries evolved as a necessity to hold the soil from falling into the lake, she is fond of Muskoka rock. "We used to love working with it." One of her favourite outings today consists of a boat trip with son Jeff, whose garden is featured elsewhere in the book, up to the head of the lake to admire the rock cliffs.

At present, Frances is in a quandary about whether to cut down a beautiful pine that grew up next to a handsome specimen of granite set in place years ago. It rises from a bed of nasturtiums, Shasta daisies, prostrate spruce, hosta, iris, pinks and sedum, anchored by a dwarf blue spruce. The grey rock, pink with white quartz on one face, "looks like a bear with two paws and a long snout. . . . Now the pine blocks the view of the rock from the cottage."

Frances Reid, with her late husband Calvin, owned a nursery in Metro Toronto. The bear rock, plus two handsome stone dogs that guard pots of geranium at a landing in the stairway, came from the business. "I ran a flower shop. Oh, the weddings. People still say to me, 'You did my wedding.' There were so many, I don't always remember. But I remember one was a complete gardenia wedding. The bouquets of gardenias trailed to the floor on ribbons."

During those busy years, the couple worked on the gardens at the cottage in whatever time they could spare, planting and tending evergreens and perennials.

Near the wrought-iron gates at the entrance to the property, workers drilled 200 feet (60 m) through a big rock for a well. Loads of topsoil were brought in to cover the upheaval and the Reids planted rhododendrons and azaleas. In the early years, they propped evergreen boughs over the plants to prevent branches breaking off under heavy snow.

Partway down the slope sits the original cottage, now known as the Penthouse. Upon their retirement in the 1970s the Reids built a larger place, near the lake.

Reid remembers those early retirement years with nostalgia. She and friends on nearby islands used to have lovely lunch parties, comparing notes on gardening. "Today we can hardly get into the boats," she says ruefully.

These days Frances Reid has help with her garden from a young woman, but remains very much a hands-on gardener. "Oh, there's a weed," she says during a walk, darting onto the

Beside spires of pink astilbe, stone dogs stand guard over the rockeries at a long-established garden.

hillside to pull the offender out by the roots. Although the hillside gardens include a prolific and fastidiously tidy vegetable garden and passing boats often slow down so passengers can admire the flowers, Frances occasionally frets that the gardens aren't what they used to be. She is, however, justifiably pleased with an impressive bed of candelabra primroses that extends about 40 feet (12 m) in one of the rockeries. "I got the first [plant] from a woman in Hamilton;

it's *Primula japonica*," with spires that rise more than a foot high in "tiers of bloom."

At the crest of the garden, between cottages, purple-leafed sandcherry contrasts with huge clumps of blue-green hosta flowing downhill like a brook. Tall phlox, foxglove, iris and great clumps of astilbe in pink, white and deep red add rich colour.

In a sunny bed by the cottage nearer the lake, she grows

hollyhocks, dwarf Shasta daisies, lupines, birds nest spruce, mauve delphiniums and sedum, accented by the annual red hot poker. Hosta, bergenia, lily of the valley and coral astilbe fill a shady border. Beside a bed bright with alyssum, white impatiens, cannas, and tuberous begonias in smashing yellow and red, stone steps lead to the boathouse.

On the boathouse deck, Frances experiments with new annuals and old favourites in containers. Purple scaevola and yellow-blooming helichrysum are combined with pink geraniums. Lime licorice plant (*Helichrysum petiolatum* Limelight) sets off a creeping portulaca with pink, yellow-centred blooms. In the fall, soil from the clay containers is tipped through a funnel into bags for the winter. The soil is used "over and over," but fertilized every week or so in the spring to put nutrients back in.

On the hillside under the shade of a tall hemlock, a planting of bergenia, pulmonaria, phlox, cedar, prostrate juniper, primula, Little Princess spirea and a dwarf blue spruce is edged by moss, arabis and sedums. Below a maple tree, fibrous begonias, cotoneaster and pink, white and red astilbe glow in the sun.

Creeping hydrangea, which has glossy leaves with flashes of white flowers, tumbles down the rock retaining walls. Frances reports that it takes about three years to get it started creeping. However, she says, for most plants, the high light intensity, including reflected light from the lake, promotes rapid growth that is almost a problem, and it's a challenge to keep plants from overcrowding.

With their enduring stonework and prodigious plantings, these Muskoka rockeries will give pleasure for years to come.

❧ THE GRAND ROCK GARDENS OF LLANLLAR ❧

The grand gardens at Llanllar, an estate on Lake Rosseau, are probably the best known in Muskoka. They include a much-admired rock garden that was one of the first of its kind in Canada.

The rock garden remains the favourite of Ted Donaldson of Windermere, who tended the gardens at Llanllar for more than half a century, starting in 1944 when he was sixteen, becoming head gardener in 1978 and retiring in May 1997.

Joseph Irwin purchased the property for a summer home on the east shore of Lake Rosseau in 1908. According to an article by Virginia Peake in the 1987 Muskoka Lakes Association yearbook, the gardens then consisted of a bed on the lawn by the bay planted to look like a Union Jack, and some hollyhocks and phlox arranged to hide the vegetable garden. Stumps filled with annuals lined the steps to the buildings.

It was Elsie Sweeney, Irwin's granddaughter, who began to design gardens. In 1926 when the idea was still a novelty in

Canada, she took a notion, as Donaldson says, to create a rock garden sloping from the house down to the lake. The project involved filling crevices with gravel for drainage and choosing alpines and low-growing perennials.

Osborne Longhurst of Windermere became head gardener around 1928, beginning a long collaboration with Sweeney. Neither had any formal training in horticulture, Peake wrote. "Miss Sweeney had an extensive library in all aspects of gardening and the two of them read, studied and experimented. They never stopped trying new methods or acquiring new and different plants. The rock garden today is breathtaking."

Before he retired, Longhurst wrote a list of plants for his successor in a yellow exercise book. It had been Sweeney's request, Longhurst reported, not to replace plants that would not winter or stand conditions in Muskoka. It took nine pages to list the plants in the rock gardens.

Among them are rock cress (*Arabis*), bugleweed (*Ajuga repens*), alyssum (*Alyssum saxatile compactum*), thrift (*Armeria*), rock aster (*Aster alpinis*), *Astilbe chinensis*, purple rock cress (*Aubretia deltoidea*), English daisy (*Bellis perennis*), bearberry (*Cotoneaster dammeri*), bellflowers (*Campanula carpatica* and *C. rotundifolia*), snow-in-summer (*Cerastium tomentosum*), daphne (*Daphne cneorum*), alpine and maiden pinks (*Dianthus alpinus* and *D. deltoides*), heath (*Erica carnea*), sneezeweed (*Helenium hoopesii*), candytuft (*Iberis*), irises, hosta, dead nettle (*Lamium*), lavender (*Lavandula*), creeping Jenny (*Lysimachia punctata*), flax (*Linum perenne*) spike gayfeather (*Liatris spictata* Blazing Star), bergamot (*Monarda fistulosa*), a blue-flowered catmint (*Nepeta mussinei*), *Oenothera missouriensis*, Japanese spurge (*Pachysandra terminalis*) *Penstemon* Rose elf, *Phlox lapie* (a dwarf white), rock soapwort (*Saponaria*), sedums, alpine spirea, Anthony Waterer spirea, and speedwell (*Veronica elegans*).

The rock garden sweeps down to a level area near the boathouse accented with a pastel planting of veronicas, pink cranesbill geraniums, lavender, sedums and pale pink Elsie Poulsen

This perennial border is maintained to a design that guarantees continuous bloom from early summer to Thanksgiving.

roses. Plants that straggle are tied up with green twine, which the late Clementine Tangeman, one of the family who took a great interest in the gardens, chose as less obtrusive than white.

An unusual primrose, *Primula polyantha* Pacific, surrounds a lamp standard; its leaves are indeed as Donaldson described, "as big as a steering wheel."

A tour by cart with Donaldson reveals his intimate knowledge of the gardens — he calls the hundreds of plants by botanical name — and memories of the landscape over fifty years. He recalls the era of kerosene lamps and the ice house, when plants were divided, how an azalea finally bloomed after he fertilized it, what it was like to move rocks before the welcome arrival of a Massey-Ferguson tractor in the mid-50s. "Osborne and I used to load rocks on the wheelbarrow and then see which of us could push 'er," he says with a chuckle.

As head gardener, Donaldson has enlisted the help of local workers who are on the property all summer doing such jobs as keeping stone pathways washed. "After Thanksgiving we get into the real work."

The secret of building a rock wall at an embankment, Donaldson advises, is to use larger flat rocks every so often and push them horizontally right into the soil of the embankment. This keeps the other rocks well balanced and level so they don't topple out over time.

In years gone by, the Irwin–Miller–Sweeney family opened a woodland valley once a week to the public for twenty-five cents a person, the proceeds going to Windermere United Church. Visitors could stroll along paths to see maidenhair and ostrich fern, hydrangeas, rhododendrons, hostas, the feathery white spires of 8-foot-tall (2.4 m) snakeroot (*Cimicefuga racemosa*), periwinkle and Japanese spurge. A stream turned on when the tourists arrived splashed its way down the ravine over waterfalls and into rock pools that held goldfish and white and blue water lilies.

On a hillside perched a Japanese teahouse. Japanese-style bridges crossed the stream, which divided to create islands. Lights shone through full-, half- and quarter-moon cut-outs in wooden lamps mounted on posts along the walks.

Unfortunately, Donaldson says, too many visitors failed to respect the request to look but not touch. Some pulled up plants to take home, a bold few lay down on the plants for an afternoon snooze. Others, told they could pick apples on the ground but not from the trees, would shake the trees until apples fell. Too many disregarded Private signs, wandering off to peer into a family dwelling "over yonder." Eventually, the tours were cancelled. Today, the descendants of Joseph Irwin continue their philanthropic tradition in many other ways and the woodland garden is returning to nature.

By the tennis courts, Donaldson stops the cart. "There's some loosestrife right there. It's all over the place." Whenever he sees it, he digs it up or lops off the top before it can go to seed.

On the lawn, the family maintains the Union Jack garden, which dates to early in the century. Various plants have been tried over the years to achieve the distinctive red in the flag and Donaldson says his choice of a fibrous begonia Vodka seems to come the closest.

A rose garden on the lawn is undergoing some renovation under the direction of the new "young lady" gardener.

Among the annuals used around the estate are tuberous begonias. Donaldson dries them, takes the stem off and transports them to Windermere Garden Centre, where they are stored for the winter and potted up the next spring.

Asked which common name he uses for aegopodium, sometimes called goutweed, Donaldson chuckles. "Al Capone, I call it." When he was learning the name, that was the easiest way to remember it. There's an all-green version of "Al Capone," he says, and a member of the family once ordered it pulled out under the impression it was poison ivy.

Animals are the biggest challenge in the gardens today, Donaldson says. Mice chew on roots, deer eat the cedar hedge and trample the andromeda, a spreading evergreen shrub, and munch on perennials such as helenium. In winter, they tramp on the snow, packing it down so it freezes deeper instead of

*The rock garden at Llanllar includes alpine plants,
low-growing perennials and Elsie Poulsen roses.*

protecting the plant roots. As protection, the gardeners put bags over the cedars and Japanese yew. Donaldson says an electric fence, built to the height of a man's hip, was set up to discourage deer. String the wires any higher and the deer could duck under.

The perennial border, designed by Sweeney and planted by Longhurst, stands close to the shore of the bay. It is backed by a magnificent green screen hiding a vegetable garden that supplies the family with onions, beets, carrots, lettuce, beans and peas grown from seed. The border blooms all summer, as flowering times overlap. A partial list includes pink astilbe, yellow heliopsis, coral bells, foxglove, purple monkshood, white and blue veronicas, white alyssum, phlox, sea campion (*Silene maritima*), asters, artemisia, yarrow, bellflowers (*Campanula compacta* and *C. persificolia*), pinks, lupine, mallow (*Sidalcea*), hardy statice (*Limonium*), foxglove, sneezeweed (*Helenium*

autumnale Bronze and *H. hoopesii*), and coneflowers (*Rudbeckia purpurea* and *R. herstonie*), hollyhocks (Blueport double pink), liatris and thyme (*Thymus saturea montana*). Donaldson points out *Clematis Davadiana*, a rare clematis that does not climb. Among the fall bloomers are *Sedum spectabile* and boltonia, which Longhurst described as "the only one of any value in September and October."

"Partly because so many people come by boat to capture the border on video cameras, we never cut the border down till after Thanksgiving," Donaldson says.

The family keeps the original plan of the perennial border mounted under glass so the garden can be maintained to Elsie Sweeney's clever design. Listening to Ted Donaldson speak with respect and affection of Miss Elsie, it is obvious that her spirit still animates the gardens.

❧ ROCKS CARPETED IN FLOWERS ❧

Participants in the annual garden tour put on by the Huntsville Horticultural Society let out sighs of admiration when they reach the Laferrière home on Mary Lake.

Sited on the crest of a steep rocky property, the log home is surrounded by rocks carpeted in flowering ground covers, beds and borders of perennials and shrubs, and a model vegetable garden. What Lorena Laferrière calls stepping things — slices of birch trunks and flat stones — form inviting paths through the gardens.

In her favourite garden to the right of the front of the house, she placed burning bush, euonymus, hosta, poppies, peach bellflower, lavender, pinks, purple beebalm and Shasta daisies. Most of these stay in the neat clump form that Laferrière prefers. She tolerates the sprawl of black-eyed Susans.

The most recent garden is evolving against the garage, faced with boards that look like barnboard but are actually planks once used to cover lumber at a mill where Gaetan Laferrière's father worked. When the mill in the Algonquin Park area burned down, Gaetan, known as Patch, rescued the weathered boards.

Parts of the garden near the garage are terraced with railway ties, to the left embracing sedum, geum, cleome, zinnias and potentilla. Enormous granite boulders, some left there after construction, have been winched and wiggled, as Lorena describes it, into locations where they will warm the soil for spring bulbs and provide attractive backgrounds for flowers in three seasons.

In one area, Lorena plants gladioli, in another, dahlias, stored in winter in the root cellar. Among the boulders shine neat clumps of moonbeam coreopsis, liatris, sweet William, sedum, a fall astilbe, giant allium, Shastas held up by a stake and plastic-coated wire, cranesbill, pink coreopsis, two hydrangea, calendula from seed, lupine, spiderwort and cosmos.

Lorena started out with a truck full of topsoil, but found it contaminated with weeds. Now she buys eight or ten bags of treated soil a year and says that at a local nursery she's known as the Triple Mix girl.

Cucumbers, lettuce, climbing peas and potatoes thrive in soil mixed with peat and manure in a prolific vegetable garden at Mary Lake.

It's hard to imagine that the property back in 1986 consisted entirely of bush and rock. The Laferrières spent six months camping out in tiny outbuildings made by hand until the shell of their year-round home went up in two weeks that summer.

They started gardening almost immediately while finishing the interior of the house. On the slope to the left, carrying rocks down in a bucket, they built a stone-walled log walkway. When soil washed out repeatedly, they eventually added drains and cemented the stone walls in place. The walkway leads down to a garden on the rocks, originally all weeds and grass that the Laferrières removed by digging down a foot past the roots. Heading to the lake for her daily swim, Lorena carried treated topsoil in a bucket to fill in the area.

Stones placed for a path are surrounded by bark chips. Goutweed, creeping thyme and yellow sedum surround a shallow lily pond. Lorena says it's wonderful to watch birds taking a bath in the pond, and when a big raccoon and two babies came by to dine on the plants, it was hard to get angry at them. The couple feed the chipmunks and leave the lid on their composter open for easy access for raccoons.

Below the deck looking out over the lake, during the hottest summer in recent years, the Laferrières dug past weeds and grass down to rock, lugging what they removed by wheelbarrow into the bush. Lorena planted creeping phlox in deep and pale pink, pink sedum, periwinkle, vinca, snow-in-summer and forget-me-nots, setting the stage for a striking show in springtime.

Golden sedum, creeping thyme, goutweed and phlox cover rock cleared of wild grasses.

Below the house, a stairway of seventy-five wooden steps leads to a path beside a gigantic overhanging rock down to the lake where Lorena takes a daily swim, spring, summer and fall. The wooden staircase recently replaced a handmade wooden ladder about 25 feet (7.5 m) long set at an angle that would make a vertigo-afflicted person faint. Lorena, her husband and her mother, Florence, thought nothing of clambering up and down the ladder, often carrying gear to and from the dock. Mercifully the new staircase features a landing with a bench for the out-of-breath.

Patch Laferrière is largely responsible for the immaculate vegetable garden, which boasts climbing peas, tomatoes, potatoes, onions, beets, lettuce, cucumbers and cantaloupes. All summer long, he says, they eat only vegetables they grow, lunching daily for three months on toasted tomato sandwiches, snacking on radish sandwiches and snap peas right off the vine.

In beds around the vegetables, Lorena planted delphiniums, yarrow, poppies, rhubarb, artemisia, black-eyed Susans, peach bellflower, columbine, snow-in-summer, Shasta daisies and roses.

Now that the garden is established, Lorena says she likely toils in it no more than an hour a day in the summer, but her husband estimates it works out to three or four. Near the garage she's working on a shade garden with hostas, including miniatures, and violets. And she has plans for expansion to the driveway area. Visitors on the annual garden tour can look forward to something new every year at this ambitious Mary Lake garden.

Compost augments the soil in this flower box bursting with nasturtiums.

CHAPTER 2

Soil

Sandy. Sparse. Poor. Rocky. Acidic. Cottage gardeners seldom have an encouraging word to say about the soil on their properties. It is, of course, perfectly good soil for wild grasses, conifers, berry bushes, ferns and other indigenous plants. But it's far from the rich loam ideal for growing cultivated ornamental plants or vegetables.

Shallow soil doesn't retain water, drying out quickly on slopes. When shallow soil rests on underlying rock, water pools in the soil, clogging air passages. Sandy soil may be easy to work, but water drains away too fast, carrying nutrients with it. Soils with a pH in the acidic range, below the neutral point of 7, affect the availability of soluble salts, resulting in stunted growth for most ornamentals. Rocky soil can be difficult to till and causes root vegetables to grow in warped shapes. Compacted soil left in the wake of heavy machinery brought in for cottage construction or renovation inhibits the circulation of air and water so that roots don't grow properly.

To control soil depth and improve drainage, some cottage gardeners construct raised beds. Another advantage to raised beds is that soil temperatures warm up sooner in the spring.

A number of cottagers bring in soil by the truckload or by barge, or lug dozens of bags of sterilized and premixed soil to their flower and vegetable beds. In considering imported topsoil, botanist Bonnie Bergsma of Muskoka cautions that it may bring with it all sorts of weed seeds that are alien to the cottage area.

Many cottagers are embracing a less expensive, although more time consuming solution, adding organic matter to the soil through composting. Organic matter increases the soil's ability to retain moisture and binds soil aggregates into a desirable granular structure that promotes circulation of water and air and holds nutrients where they're needed near the roots. It also contains microorganisms helpful to plants.

Composting, of course, reduces the amount of garbage sent to dumps. Local governments and most taxpayers are aware that dump sites are running out and that tax dollars can be better spent than on hauling away mounds of vegetable waste. Composting also fits the cottagers' traditional do-it-yourself ethos and brings an innate satisfaction from working with a renewable resource in nature.

Next to composting, the best soil strategy for the cottage gardener is mulching. Any material placed on the soil to conserve moisture, raise the soil temperature and discourage weeds will do — black polyethylene film, stones or gravel, bark or other organic material. Mulch should be placed in a 2- to 3-inch (5–7 cm) layer. Neither hay nor straw is recommended because either attracts mice and voles.

One should mulch with caution. Never mulch with lawn clippings that have been treated against broad-leafed weeds; these chemicals will harm deciduous shrubs, perennials and flowering annuals. Don't place mulch too near trees; it conceals rodents that will chew on the bark. Mulch around, not on top of, the crowns of perennials. Don't mulch too early in the spring or the mulch will insulate the soil from the sun's rays.

The cottagers in this chapter import desirable soil or create it by using materials at hand, such as leaves and compost, a technique that is inexpensive and friendly to the environment. Without amendments to the soil, the successful cultivation of the range of plants chosen by these gardeners would be impossible.

❦ COMPOSTING FOR CONTAINERS ❦

Having spent summers at the same cottage for fifty years, Helen Boggild appreciates tradition, yet she's open to fresh ideas for the garden.

Recently she became a convert to composting. Although she had originally brought in soil to fill raised beds over the rock, the routine of buying soil to fill flower boxes for annuals "seemed ridiculous." Composting is a conservation effort, she says, and besides, she resents wasting food scraps. She has joined the Muskoka Heritage Foundation, a charitable foundation that encourages conservation through private stewardship.

In the case of the herb vinegars and jellies for which she is famous in her family, Helen experiments with novel ingredients. She clips the brilliant red fruits of sumac from the hillside and makes sumac jelly, "the poor man's red currant." Her opal basil vinegar shimmers with a cranberry light in its tall glass bottle; chive vinegar of a faint lavender hue swirls around chive blossoms and leaves floating upright in another bottle. "The family joke is if anything stands still, I'll make jelly out of it or paint it."

Helen likes reading about the old values assigned to herbs and the uses of herb medicines and concoctions. For her birthday, a niece gave her a large terra-cotta pot inscribed "Hunny's Herbs," Hunny being Helen's nickname. One summer it held dill and three kinds of basil. "Herbs grow beautifully in pots," Helen observes, "because you can move them."

Dill, three kinds of basil, parsley and mint in terra cotta pots are destined for garnishes, jellies and herb vinegars.

Containers also control the spread of herbs that tend to be invasive. Recently she ripped up most of the mint in the flower beds and planted it in a basket. Among her mints is ginger mint (*Mentha x. gentilis Variegata*), which has gold-flecked leaves.

Although Helen has planted many a window box in the classic geranium-petunia-ivy trio for the boathouse, in other containers she now sometimes uses parsley, combined perhaps with lobelia and zinnias. "Who needs ivy? You get a lovely frilly look with parsley."

In the composted soil of a window box on the porch over-looking the lake, Helen began a few years ago planting nasturtiums — profusion of tumbling red, orange and yellow. "I look at colour as to how it blends with the old cottage, and use warm colours against the brown," she says, "and I love trailing lobelia — that blue is marvellous."

By the classic screen door to the cottage, Helen tried the evergreen shrub Oregon grape (*Mahonia aquifolium*), against the advice of friends who said it would not be hardy in Muskoka. In this sheltered sunny spot, its yellow flowers warm the brown wood.

Animals haven't been a bother in her garden, except for a black bear that knocked down the hummingbird feeder and left huge pawprints on the window — "our fourth bear" over the years.

She buys annuals, but may yet start growing them from seed; she's been saving an old window "for years" to use as a cold frame. "Most of our plants have come from my father's garden and my sister's," she says. Her father, Ted Hartwick, donated old-fashioned pale pink roses and orange and yellow day-lilies from his log cabin around the bay near Horseshoe Island on Lake Muskoka. Her late sister Marjorie provided "a poppy which I love and a few bits of *Campanula persificolia*. She inspired me to plant rhododendrons; hers were magnificent." Helen mulches them with pine needles to maintain the acidic soil they need and covers them with pine boughs for the winter.

In her flower bed above the cottage, Helen planted astilbe, fern, yellow lilies, a burning bush (*Euonymus alatus*) and buttercups. Vinca minor grows near ferns, hosta, pink lilies, Froebel's spirea and the meadow plant herb Robert (*Geranium robertianum*). Lupines, red and white astilbe, lady's mantle and lamb's ears — "the bees love them" — bloom in July. A friend gave her "Helen's flower," which looks like a small gaillardia in orange, yellow and brown. She uses creeping Jenny and snow-on-the-mountain as ground covers. In some beds, she puts leaf lettuce, both decorative and edible.

Helen is amused at the appearance of a mullein, a tall pasture weed, that sprouted uninvited in the garden. "I get hysterical every time I look at it." Although she gardens in raised beds, "the forest has a way of creeping in that pleases me."

Petunias and lobelia accent the screen door at this Lake Muskoka cottage. A stray mullein, left, self-seeded.

She points to a birdbath, a find from the Muskoka Arts and Crafts Show. "That's my grave," she says, indicating a spot below where she wants her ashes laid to rest. "Well, it will make good compost for the garden."

Helen Boggild spends every possible moment at the cottage from springtime, when the natural flora — trilliums, lady's slipper and moccasin flower — spread all down the hillside to the lake. "It's such a joy to have continuous bloom and no responsibility." In the autumn when the leaves are falling, she has to be "pried away" from the cottage.

❧ ADDING THE MAGIC OF LEAVES ❧

An experienced gardener at a Haliburton cottage used leaves and newspapers to solve a challenge with soil.

Marion Robinson has gardened at home and since 1964 at cottages in Haliburton. At a previous cottage on Horseshoe Lake she found the soil fertile and easy to keep moist. But when she and Jim bought their present property at Duck Lake, the hillside where she envisaged a perennial garden wouldn't hold water.

A forested slope, broken only by the clearing for hydro poles, came right down to pavement behind the cottage. The Robinsons cleared some trees and positioned tiers of rock in the hillside. Then Marion dug a trench behind each rock ledge and buried newspapers and leaves. As they decomposed, the organic matter helped form soil that retains moisture even on the hottest days.

At first Marion planted just above the pavement but gradually she expanded the garden outward and up. Rhubarb that once marked the end of the garden now sits near the centre. Today the garden boasts a rainbow of diverse perennials, augmented by annuals such as nasturtiums, pansies and snapdragons.

Hosta, phlox, yarrow, daisies, two kinds of mint and lily of the valley grow at one end, with beebalm and crimson lilies placed near the rock stairs that divide the garden. On the other side, phlox, gloriosa daisies, lupines, veronica, delphiniums, Canterbury bells, beebalm, lungwort, campanula and cranesbill geranium guarantee a show of

flowers with plants successively in bloom all summer. In mid-August, delicate blue love-in-a-mist (*Nigella damascena*) contrasts with the warmer colours on display.

In the spring, narcissi and daffodils bloom as early at the cottage as they do in her city garden 125 miles to the southwest. "It's very hot here because of the sun on the hillside," Robinson notes. "I use a lot of leaves each fall to cover the perennials and try to leave [the mulch] there in the spring."

In 1996 she started a vegetable garden at a right angle to the perennials. Although there is no direct sun on that area until noon, the vegetable garden was an instant success, with plants well advanced by early August. For this garden, the Robinsons brought in topsoil and added leaves — "a lot." Swiss chard, dill, onions, cucumbers, squash and kohlrabi are accented at one end by pink dahlias that shot up 5 1/2 feet (1.5 m) in the leaf-enriched soil, reminding Robinson of sugar cane. Pole beans and scarlet runner beans climb attractive supports handmade of cedar.

Enriched by leaves, the soil in a wooden container produces a harvest of spectacular tomatoes.

The Robinson's cottage, built in 1974 as an executive retreat by an American company, came on the market a decade later, complete with furniture, linens and fishing rods. The property included title to 10,000 feet (3,000 m) of shoreline, almost the entire circumference of the lake. Two families of relatives have become neighbours on the secluded spring-fed lake.

With so much forested land all around, Marion enjoys identifying the native plants of Haliburton, such as a purple-flowering raspberry (*Rubus odoratus*) growing out of a rock crevice on the path down to the lake.

Outside the front door, a lawn provides a level spot for enjoying refreshments or taking part in "roll-a-ball," a sort of lawn bowling that appeals to all ages, from Jim Robinson's former colleagues to the couple's lively young grandchildren. A designated judge settles any disputes from a perch on a tractor seat on the slope above the lawn.

Beside the dock where a cement ramp once served as a boat launch site, the Robinsons recently constructed a large rectangular container for flowers. They harvest sunflower seeds to feed birds at home in the winter.

Along the shore where the sun shines all day, Jim built sturdy wooden containers for tomato plants. Because Marion was concerned that fertilizer chemicals might leach into the lake, Jim lined the boxes with heavy plastic. They threw leaves into the boxes and brought soil down the slope on an all-terrain vehicle. Each year, they add more leaves to the soil.

Marion starts the plants from seed at home under glass. When frost threatens in the fall, they cover the crop with tarpaulins. "It's a shame to lose them when the next frost might not come for two weeks," she says. They grow three kinds of tomatoes — Early Boy, beefsteak and a long-lasting variety that they store on newspaper in the basement at home. The long-lasting tomatoes lived up to their name the first year, Marion reported. "We ate the last one on Good Friday."

At the lakeside, Marion also tends a unique short-season garden. The previous owners had set shallow flat rocks into the hillside, forming a terrace that looked ideal for a garden. But when she planted the area she discovered that it was an established egg-laying habitat for turtles. Other animals move in to dig up the eggs, uprooting plants, especially annuals, in the process.

"One year I planted three times in the spring, then I smartened up," she says. "I can't plant this till the first of July."

Adding water weeds to provide extra nutrients to the soil, she makes a colourful display at the lakeside with yellow

If this lakeside spot is planted before July, animals digging for turtle eggs uproot the plants.

yarrow, phlox, coreopsis, gloriosa daisies, milkweed and lilies of a rich, almost brown hue. And, she observes, the broken eggshells enrich the soil.

Pottery name tags identify some thirty herbs, from angelica to stachys,
at a garden that stretches the limits at Georgian Bay. A rattlesnake resides nearby.

🌿 GIFTS FOR A GARDENER 🌿

Every year for her birthday, Elizabeth Bryce receives fifty bags of topsoil for her six cottage gardens. Her husband, Douglas, has found the perfect gift for a serious gardener. Some of the birthday soil goes into old wooden boats, which Elizabeth uses as containers. Elsewhere she piles soil into natural rock crevices.

Her reputation as the doyenne of gardening in the Georgian Bay islands off Pointe-au-Baril is formidable; her neighbours tend to say, "Well, yes, I grow things, but nothing like Libby Bryce, of course."

Near the shoreline, where cedars, pin cherry and pine trees offer natural protection from the west wind, Elizabeth planted her first and most spectacular boat garden. The garden now extends beyond the boat, but the bow can still be seen through soil that has built up inside and around the hull.

Elizabeth enjoys the "smash" of delphiniums in the boat garden. Her Blue Boy and Black Knight delphiniums accent the Shasta daisies, autumn sedum, veronica, lavender, pyrethrum, Jacob's ladder, phlox, tansy, lysimachia, loosestrife, prince's feathers, cranesbill geranium and lovage. Oriental and Asiatic lilies and daylilies are chosen for a succession of bloom all summer. "I leave a border of artemisia because it highlights the colour, but you have to watch it" so it doesn't take over, she says.

Goldenrod, sumac and juniper sweep naturally to the side of the cultivars. Farther out toward the bay, she planted willows to screen the view of a neighbour's cottage built where the family was used to seeing rock and water.

Taking after her mother, Elizabeth Bryce has "always gardened." She joined the Garden Club of Toronto in 1958, later serving as president. She's also a past president of the Herb Society of North America.

It would be difficult to imagine a more extensive herb garden at a cottage, and Elizabeth had a plant list at the ready. Her herbs aren't chosen specifically for dyes, culinary use or fragrance, but for "whatever will grow." In her experienced hands that includes basil, opal basil, fennel, rue, rosemary, French tarragon, calendula, marjoram, Greek oregano, bergamot, angelica, lovage, sweet Cicely, salad burnet, dianthus, sage, lychnis, golden sage, parsley. There are two lavenders, Hidcote and Munstead, *Rosa mundi*, golden oregano, lemon thyme, lady's mantle, two scented geraniums, and two species of stachys — betony and lamb's ears (*Stachys lanata*). She finds basil does better in a tub than in the garden. A second tub holds pineapple mint and Italian parsley.

For Christmas one year, her daughter and daughter-in-law combined talents, one fashioning pottery name tags for the herbs, one writing the names in calligraphy. Elizabeth contrived an ingenious supporting fence of silvery grey cedar branches covered by golden hops vine for the herb garden. As it's being admired, she warns casually, "Do watch out for rattlesnakes."

The Bryces' daughter was married at the cottage. The main cottage was once a Roman Catholic chapel; sleeping

The chapel garden, one of six perennial displays, benefits from topsoil added each spring.

quarters are in separate buildings. Wedding guests strolled by the front chapel garden with its white lupine, red peony, Shasta daisies, phlox, orange "Twelfth of July" lilies, astilbe, marjoram, loosestrife, prince's feather, sedum, oriental lilies, pink and yellow yarrow, Silver King artemisia, annual cosmos and biennial lavatera. Outside the chapel a platform of planks on half-cut logs held the receiving line and served as a dance floor.

To the right of the chapel, her son-in-law later heaved huge rocks to make a surround for a rose garden. A Thérèse Bugnet rose lasts through the winter and Bryce brings fourteen or fifteen less hardy roses to the island every year. On the shore side of the chapel in the shade, she planted astilbe and Japanese painted fern.

In the front boat garden against a backdrop of cedar and fern, she grows daylilies, sedum, anthemis, yarrow, gaillardia, double coreopsis, and the annuals marigold, impatiens and nicotiana. "If you plant enough there's no room for weeds," she says.

Adjacent to a tennis court there are more perennials — delphinium, alchemilla, sedum, yellow and blue lupine, pink gaillardia, white Shasta daisies, orange and yellow daylilies, steeple bush, chives, blue globe thistle (*Echinops*), loosestrife, rudbeckia, sweet William, veronica, anthemis and phlox. Cosmos, marigolds, and blue salvia, which is not hardy in Zone 4, spider plant (*Cleome*) and strawflowers are added as annuals.

When summer ends, many of Elizabeth Bryce's flowers and herbs enter a second incarnation in dried flower arrangements. In the spring, the birthday bags of soil signal the start of another season at this celebrated Georgian Bay garden.

❧ One Wheelbarrow at a Time ❧

In the still of the early morning, George Woerner takes a coffee to the glider seat at the top of the rock to watch the lake. A loon pops up and fish make circles while yellow finches flit overhead. Between the glider seat and the lake lies the garden in the rocks, which his neighbours say is the most photographed spot on spring-fed Horseshoe Lake in the district of Parry Sound.

Laudia Woerner says her husband spent every weekend for eight summers working at the cottage garden on the point of their 700 feet (210 m) of shoreline. When she asked if he wasn't overdoing it, he maintained that gardening helped him forget the stress of work in the city.

The first big task, he recalls, was bringing soil across to the property, which is accessible only by water. Two tractor-trailer loads were transported, the first in a 16-foot boat, the second by barge, and carted up the rocks by George and sons Paul, then fourteen, and Trevor, then twelve, one wheelbarrow load at a time.

With the first load he replaced the poor soil, which was composed of oak leaves and pine needles in rock crevices; with the second he made a 12-foot (4 m) planting bed at the one flat spot beside the rock face. He aimed for 12 to 16 inches (25–40 cm) of soil to sustain the plantings.

George left in place some native plants such as juniper, grasses and blueberry bushes, trimming them occasionally, but with the idea that cottage gardens aren't meant to replicate the manicured look of those in the city. He likes to experiment with different cultivars. Plants that suited conditions at the cottage came up again; others died out. Sedums, yellow and red, hen and chickens, and creeping phlox did well on the rock face, and near the top he put in euonymus and rugged rugosa roses, which bloom at least three times in this location and are sending up new shoots.

The wind, particularly a strong north wind, can be a problem. Lupines that come up beautifully are knocked flat. George has found that plants with heavy blossoms, such as peonies, are best grown in the city where they are more sheltered. At the cottage, he favours intermediate to short plants, as they are less vulnerable to wind damage. Nevertheless, in a more sheltered place right against the rock, he planted sunflowers one year, staking them for support. The heads grew to 18 inches (45 cm) across and the birds loved them, the bluejays scattering the seeds around the property where the chipmunks collected them.

In the sunny main bed, heliopsis, painted daisies, black-eyed Susans, Maltese cross, poppies, pinks, lupines, marguerites, blanketflowers, *Geum* Mrs. Bradshaw, blue speedwell, cornflowers, three types of phlox and baby's breath make a colourful picture.

Further up the hill, blueberries, daisies and clover grow under a purple-martin house.

In shady spots, George placed begonias, coleus and some pinks, and by the glider, basket-of-gold, a Froebel spirea, hosta and cotoneaster. Elsewhere he had luck with soapwort, zinnias, sweet William and orange daylilies. He maintains that continuous fertilizing is the secret of summer-long bloom, particularly for annuals in tubs and hanging pots.

Nearer the cottage, native plants such as bluebead lily and bearberry grow undisturbed. A septic bed was seeded with a wildflower mix, which he waters once in a while. In the main beds he put in a soaker hose and sprinklers, timed to come on early in the morning each day.

George keeps his fingers crossed that a city of groundhogs, which had made over twenty holes in his neighbour's hill when he first bought the cottage, have gone for good. With the neighbour's permission, George stuffed rocks and branches in

Tons of soil brought by boat and barge across Horseshoe Lake in the district of Parry Sound
formed the base for these gardens.

the holes and set up a battery-operated system that emitted a high-pitched sound every minute or so. Since the third summer, he hasn't seen a groundhog.

One year, however, a bear visited in late winter and helped itself to seed in the bird feeders, breaking them in the process. Although the Woerners like to watch the hummingbirds,

grosbeaks, phoebes and goldfinches, they decided not to replace the feeders.

There was a time, George Woerner says, when he couldn't understand the attractions of cottage life. Now the family is planning to erect a permanent home at Horseshoe Lake.

Soil is the main challenge at a Stony Lake cottage, where the owner mixes old favourites with exotic annuals.

❧ STONY LAKE FRIENDSHIP GARDEN ❧

In Kathy Dembroski's garden between the boathouse and the cottage, the plants are all labelled — but not with botanical names. This is her Friendship Garden; each plant's marker proclaims the name of the friend who gave her the plant.

Kathy jokes that when she's asking people to the cottage on Stony Lake in the Kawarthas, she tells them the invitation is conditional on bringing her a root from their gardens.

When she's working in that garden with the lupines, delphiniums, bachelor buttons, coneflowers, snow-on-the-mountain, astilbe, woolly thyme, white veronica, lilies, yarrow, phlox and obedient plant, she thinks of the friends. "Here's Julie Medland's artemisia," she says fondly. To her friends' contributions she adds annuals such as cleomes, datura,

poppies, nicotiana, and bells of Ireland, a plant with apple-green bracts on the stem. Large rocks brought up in the construction of the boathouse have also been incorporated into the Friendship Garden.

On the other side of the walkway leading to the boathouse, Kathy put in a box of plants including poppies and phlox, and verbena, sedum, hostas, cornflower, artemisia, nicotiana and bergenia. By the boathouse, she planted *Astilbe chinensis*, bright yellow heliopsis and *Stephanandra incisa crispa*, a shrub with fernlike leaves that will grow in sun or partial shade in any soil.

Her biggest challenge is the soil, bringing it to the island and keeping it rich enough to grow the kinds of plants she wants.

Although she's the gardener of the family, her husband, George, does much of the heavy work and has shown interest in the restoration of a herb garden, particularly when the produce goes into stuffing a chicken full of herbs before baking it. In her new herb garden she elevates some of the plants, such as winter savory and parsley, by placing them in hollow stumps filled with soil. She also grows dill, purple basil, angelica and garlic chives.

Kathy, who calls herself a "flower freak," is now reviving two original flower beds that were ringed with rocks. In one of the gardens, she planted liatris, lysimachia, bergamot, coneflower, phlox, lupines, marguerites, tiger lilies and blue thistle. In a wildflower garden, she encourages Queen Anne's lace, daisies, black-eyed Susans, yarrow and sedums.

In planters on the back deck, she grows summer hyacinth, bells of Ireland, datura, ivy, snapdragon and lavatera. She also places containers on the dock below the front of the cottage but doesn't keep as many on the verandah these days because of wind. The Dembroskis' cottage, purchased in 1984, is a turn-of-the-century two-storey building with a wide verandah. With the help of old photos, they carefully restored the exterior to its earlier appearance.

Kathy says she finds a growing interest in gardening among cottagers. She has decided to exchange plants between her gardens at home and at the cottage, bringing summer-flowering plants to the cottage and taking home plants that bloom in late spring.

Kathy Dembroski has been busy for several years coordinating Canada Blooms, an international flower show she initiated to celebrate the 50th anniversary of the Garden Club of Toronto and the 25th anniversary of Landscape Ontario in 1997. And so her love of flowers, as epitomized in the Friendship Garden, has reached out to benefit a much wider group of plant enthusiasts.

PERSEVERING WITH VEGETABLES

Despite deer, drought, wind, rain, and obligations that take him away from the garden, Timothy Regan has been growing vegetables on Ojibway Island for twenty-five years.

He began the first garden near the main cottage by bringing soil from the mainland out to the island in Georgian Bay. He laid out the garden to conserve precious earth. Raised beds are divided by wooden planks laid on edge, with small white stones forming pathways between the planks. Reflecting his growing expertise, his second garden is "all found earth," with added peat moss, manure and constant composting.

The raised beds hold a profusion of celery, tomatoes, several kinds of beets, different varieties of lettuce that produce continually all summer, cabbages and turnips. "We had a very early crop of broccoli." He has tried various locations for his corn, finding it a challenge to locate a patch that's sunny all day.

The deer took out the last of the basil, he notes, but in general, herbs such as sage, dill and oregano, once introduced, go on forever. Before he put up a fence to discourage hares, raccoon and deer, deer ate every plant. Raccoons will still go over the fence.

Timothy buys starter plants rather than growing from seed, because the season at the cottage is short. Once Georgian Bay warms up around the island, it holds the frost at bay at least until September. He's only lost a crop to frost once. As the sun grows progressively weaker, however, "the tomatoes give up," so he uses a food dryer to ripen them. He has installed a

Lettuce, onions, tomatoes, beets and cabbages are among the produce harvested from this faithfully tended plot on Ojibway Island.

sprinkler system to protect against droughts of up to thirty days that occur some years and play havoc with the garden.

A south vegetable garden planted in crevices on the rocky shore gets the most sun, so the soil there tends to be warmer. Obviously this is the best place for squash, Timothy says, and he also grows zucchini and melons that sprawl along the rocks at this spot.

His mother-in-law, Helen Phelan, is responsible for the flowers on the property, particularly geraniums in containers. Gail Regan says the vegetable garden is entirely her husband's project and she is delighted his efforts are being recognized. "The key to good vegetables," Timothy Regan advises, "is having the pot boiling" before you pick.

❧ BY BARGE TO CHRISTMAS ISLAND ❧

During a summer weekend up to a hundred boats circle the island that the captain of R.M.S. *Segwun* calls the most extensively landscaped on Lake Muskoka. It's not unusual for boaters sighting someone on shore to shout above the noise of the engines, "We love your flowers!" To some of the family the attention is intrusive, but Margo McGregor is delighted when people appreciate the effort she and her husband, Rod, put into the landscape on Christmas Island.

Each year she orders 10,000 annuals, planted by the supplier, and she's increasing the perennial beds as well. An order that large means she has to decide on a colour scheme in the fall. Behind the boathouse she sets an experimental bed where she assesses colour combinations. One year she planted beebalm, phlox and impatiens to see how red, fuchsia, orange and white worked together.

"I don't think there's such a thing as flowers that clash," Margo says firmly. "I tend to like bold things best. . . . Yellow is wonderful from the lake."

Below the cottage, a Frank Lloyd Wright design, the whole eastern end of the island blazes with colour. Flower beds curve around to the south shore where containers of jewel-coloured annuals bedeck the docks and boathouse. The sunset garden is situated on a western exposure. At twelve spots along the shoreline around the rest of the wooded 25 acres (10 ha), the couple established raised containers for plants left over from their main flower beds.

When, after years of admiring Christmas Island, Rod and Margo McGregor bought it in the early '90s, they knew they wanted flowers — and masses of them. They purchased a barge to carry soil and plants from the mainland. They spent so much time at Christmas Island that they sold their city home and now live six months in Muskoka and the other six in Florida. Avid golfers, the McGregors installed golf greens on the island. They like to get out on the greens when entertaining friends.

On the eastern end of Christmas Island, a bed of white and red begonias backs clumps of daylilies. Pink, purple and white coneflowers, gloriosa daisies, white astilbe and Shasta daisies wave in the breeze on the slope to the cottage with pink mallow (*Sidalcea*), liatris and hostas in front and bidens, cleome and petunias nearer the shore.

Yellow bidens, fuchsia surfinia and white and purple petunias with tall Blitz impatiens flower near the beach on the south side of the island. Pink, red and yellow tuberous begonias are bordered by blue lobelia. Gigantic orange, red, gold and rust zinnias mix with cleome. A recent bed includes begonias, alyssum, a new portulaca and marigolds.

The south garden makes a vivid show with daisies, blue delphiniums that bloom twice, lilies, liatris, phlox, dahlias, upright lobelia, spike speedwell, scabiosa, zinnias and petunias, annual and perennial salvia.

The McGregors are also working on a shade garden, starting with ferns dug up in a marsh. "Rod and I work every day all day in the garden," Margo says. "We're equally involved." It's too massive a job for one person, she declares.

Paths wind around the island, some wide enough for golf carts. The McGregors each take a buggy in the morning, work in a separate garden and meet at 11:30 for lunch. They garden again until 4 or 4:30, when they go for a boat cruise.

Margo says her style of gardening is "wild and woolly," while her husband is much more particular and likes everything neat and tidy. "He goes crazy when he sees a weed." One of the beauties of an island, she says, is that once you get rid of existing weeds you don't have the same problem. And you can plant according to sun exposure.

Soil is the most important ingredient in their gardens. "Many, many" barge-loads of soil have gone into the flower beds. Margo buys a ready-mixed soil, believing if you put a one-dollar plant in a ten-dollar hole you will have success and if you put a ten-dollar plant in a one-dollar hole you won't.

Although they have an automatic watering system, she waters by hand as well, always fertilizing with a 20-20-20 combination. "The way I feed them I need to plant seven feet apart," she jokes.

The sunset garden, the first they put in, was started with Promix and topsoil for a base. On one side of the path they planted sweet woodruff, goatsbeard, yellow lilies, hydrangea, astilbe, hosta, phlox, delphiniums, sedum and coralbells with cleome. On the other side, vinca, sedum, miniature Shastas, pampas grass, lavender, pinks and astilbe give a cool look. Massive rock chairs installed by the original owner face west for the perfect view of magnificent Muskoka sunsets.

"We have wonderful times," says Margo McGregor. "I can hardly wait till next year."

Magenta, white, orange and yellow mingle in beds where 10,000 annuals are planted each year.

❦ RICHES OF THE EARTH ❦

The hidden ingredient in the harmonious gardens at Hideaway Island is the soil — rich, fertile, and all developed right on the island with leaves and compost.

With a lush perennial bed at the shoreline, borders that complement the 1886 wooden cottage, a spring wildflower garden, a vegetable plot, and a dazzling display of nearly eight hundred annuals, it's understandable that these gardens were the most frequently recommended for this book.

In the mid-'70s when the Peakes bought Hideaway and its companion, Zurich Island, Virginia Peake identified two kinds of soil. In existing beds of yellow iris with maroon stripes, field daisies and peonies, she found a solid clay that had either been brought to the island or dug out of the lake. Elsewhere, where she wanted to establish new beds, she had to work with thin, sparse subsoil.

Instead of bringing topsoil to the island, Virginia, an experienced gardener and longtime member of the Garden Club of Toronto, with the help of her husband and sons, obtained a shredder to grind up leaves, added sheep or cow manure to the beds every year, and began composting in earnest.

"We compost everything from the kitchen and garden, including weeds not at the seed stage, raw eggshells, coffee grounds, newspaper — colour pages, just black and white — and kitty litter. If you take the solids out, it's good for adding nitrogen. Raccoons do have a look at it, so rather than have them pry the lid off [the composter], we leave it loose."

Creating soil in this way takes

The soil for spectacular perennial beds was created entirely at Hideaway Island with shredded leaves, manure and compost.

patience. When her son David started building up the soil for a vegetable patch on Zurich Island, "it took three years before he could grow anything." His fenced plot now provides tomatoes, zucchini, carrots, beets and lettuce, many of the vegetables grown from seed.

In the fall, all the planters are taken to a compost heap, turned over and dumped out. Her sons then cover it with a tarpaulin because they don't want rain and melting snow running through and leaching out the nutrients. The planters are put away in the boathouse or under the cottage for the winter. Come spring, they are refilled from the compost heap and carried to their locations on a bridge joining the two islands and on the docks and boathouse for planting.

"I grow all my own annuals," says Virginia. "It's not difficult but it is time-consuming." She spoons a sterile, soilless mix into thirty-two pans with four dozen six-packs in each pan, starting petunias in early April, lobelia next, and snapdragons, marigolds and zinnias last. She grows them under lights in the garage, where there's no room these days for anything but garden things. "What I need is a commercial greenhouse," she acknowledges with a smile. The seedlings are then transported to Lake Rosseau, the last leg of the trip by boat, with help from her understanding sons, Michael, David, Sean and Geoffrey.

At one time, she planted fifty-six containers but has scaled down to thirty or so. David, a carpenter, made the wooden ones. She doesn't wear gloves while gardening. "I have to work hands in the soil." To

All annuals were grown from seed for theses classic flower boxes.
Upright geraniums go at the back, trailing geraniums at the front, and zinnias, lobelia, snapdragons, marigolds and brachychome in between.

plant the containers, she begins with "the backbone" geraniums (*Pelargonium*) in a coral shade, then adds trailing geraniums at the front. She usually combines coral with white, blue and a touch of yellow. Two favourite zinnias are Peter Pan and a pink one called Dasher, but she also grows an African zinnia with small gold blooms. Lobelia and *Brachycome iberidifolia* give a tint of blue.

Upstairs on the brown-shingled boathouse, wooden window boxes hold blue and white petunias and trailing pink geraniums.

Near the house, Virginia and son David created a spring shade garden of trilliums, ferns, primula, cranesbill geraniums of pale blue, violets, bleeding heart, lungwort, and epimedium, which has spurred flowers.

Beside the broad wooden steps at the front of the classic, beautifully preserved old cottage, she planted hydrangeas, astilbe and bluebead lily, and to the left, ostrich ferns, hostas and tuberous begonias, which she has had for years. She digs them up with everything attached, allows them to ripen, cleans them and leaves them in peat moss in a cool place, and brings them out in March or early April to repot. Under a maple in front of the cottage, she grows hosta, lady fern and painted Japanese fern.

Virginia says groundhogs have not appeared on the island, although there was a jackrabbit once, and voles go in cycles. The Peakes have not seen deer recently, but they have noticed big scratches they attribute to a bear. "On Hideaway, we don't trap, don't shoot, and don't put out bait."

In a stunning freeform perennial bed along the Lake Rosseau shore, Peake succeeds in growing plants that will bloom in waves from May to September. The thyme along the edge came from Llanllar, the estate featured elsewhere in this book. The late Osborne Longhurst, longtime gardener at Llanllar, also gave her a heritage rose. The perennial bed boasts campanula, Shasta daisies, both blue and white veronica, snapdragons, purple bellflower, rudbeckia, phlox, sundrops, astilbe, a Thumbelina daylily with little orange flowers, hosta, and lady's mantle. Lady's mantle "can be a pest [spreading too freely] but I don't mind as long as it minds itself."

Lilies, chives, sweet woodruff, roses and a blue aster with a yellow centre that will bloom all summer grow further along in the bed. A golden yellow St. John's wort (*Hypericum*) adds to the colour along the shore.

"I let things that escape, like Johnny-jump-ups, seed themselves." With the southeast exposure, "It all sort of leans out toward the lake," Virginia Peake notes.

Upstairs in the cottage, David Peake installed window frames he made from mahogany and panes on which he sandblasted his drawings of plants that grow wild on Hideaway Island, including Dutchman's breeches, black-eyed Susans, Jack-in-the-pulpit and foamflower. They're a perfect tribute to a cottager who declares "Gardening, that's a reason for living."

Evergreens near the shore protect these pole beans from winds whistling in off Georgian Bay.

44

Chapter 3

Wind

Although major windstorms are rare, some cottage gardens are situated in the path of steady winds that dessicate the soil and plants and snap off all but the sturdiest stems. Gardeners at such cottages need to find or create protected places in which they can nurture their plants.

Prevailing winds in Central Ontario blow from the west, northwest or southwest, with southwest predominating. Winds are lightest in the summer and strongest in winter and spring. At the crest of hills, wind speeds can be 20 percent greater than at the foot of the hill.

Look for a microclimate for the garden. It might be on the lee side of shrubs, southeast of a big tree or rock, or found at an angle in a cottage that is sunny and protected from the wind. One gardener has taken advantage of the stone wall of her cottage to site a border protected from wind. Another cottager at an especially windy site gardens away from the lake, in open spots in the forest, where trees break most of the wind. Areas such as this may be slow to warm up, however, as cold air will flow over a forest and then swoosh down into an opening.

For gardeners directly in the path of heavy winds, screening becomes a matter of urgency. Wind coming up against an obstruction will arc around it. The area right behind the windbreak has lower air pressure, so in the winter snow tends to build up, insulating plants from damaging freeze-thaw-freeze cycles. When making a living windbreak, a combination of deciduous and evergreen plants is best, say, a dense plant such as potentilla and perhaps a dogwood,

ninebark and a mugho pine, with its tips or candles snipped to give it density. For every yard (metre) you go up with a windbreak, you get between 8 and 10 yards (about 8–10 m) of horizontal protection. If you picture a snow fence, which has spaces wider than its slats, an ideal windbreak would be a bit more dense, with about 60 percent of the area covered. White cedar by itself, for example, does not make a good windbreak because it is too dense. If you have lots of space, a windbreak should have some depth, not just a single row. Gardeners in this chapter have constructed windbreaks of willow trees and rock walls.

Since wind dries out soil and plants, gardeners in windy areas have to be particularly careful to ensure an adequate supply of moisture. Some have set up drip watering systems and one pumped up the water-retaining capacity of the soil with leaves and newspapers.

Plants that hug the ground, such as sedums and prostrate evergreens, and plants that bend with the wind, such as wild iris, will withstand even strong gales. For gardens not in the steady path of strong winds but subject to severe summer storms, staking tall plants can make the difference between partial damage and devastation.

Finding and creating microclimates, screening with living or solid material, compensating for drying winds with well-designed watering systems, and choosing plants that can survive a gale are the techniques that empower cottagers to garden at windy sites.

🌿 TREES AS WINDBREAK 🌿

When the west wind roars across Georgian Bay from Manitoulin, a few rocky islands and half-submerged shoals form the only break before the wind buffets the outer islands off Pointe-au-Baril.

The wind is certainly a factor in gardening, says Jim Tait, who does most of the planting at the family cottage on Empress Island. He has observed that in these windy conditions plants for window boxes do best if put in when they are small. They seem to adapt by growing compact and robust stems, bracing themselves against the wind. Full-grown bedding plants transplanted to a windy location snap in pieces at the first big blow. Jim hasn't built any windbreaks, relying on what nature provides: trees.

Most of the planting is done on the east side of the cottage in crevices and basins in the rocks. Soil on the island is sparse. Almost anywhere you dig, you find it matted with roots. In one rocky basin near the cottage, Jim dumped in earth and planted flowers. But before long they were smothered by tree roots. Recently, he filled in the bottom of the basin with concrete, creating a giant planter. A stone cairn he built to support a sundial stands nearby. And the soil tends to be acidic. Indeed, Jim gauges the acidity by the presence of American sorrel, a plant with white flowers and leaves like clover that thrives in a soil pH of just 4 to 5.

To increase the number of kinds of plants that would grow on the island, Jim and Adrienne Tait lugged soil in garbage bags by boat over many seasons. Recently they have been using up earth left over from a new septic bed installation. The soil is enriched with compost; Adrienne says that they have been composting on the island for more than thirty years. One summer they found a potato plant growing in the compost and on Thanksgiving weekend harvested a great bucketful of white potatoes.

Chicken wire encircles the vegetable garden to discourage rabbits. Jim grows tomatoes, pruning the suckers, and pole beans, particularly prolific Blue Lake. A good crop can be harvested from plants climbing up three or four poles. He also grows chives and mint, which they use for sauce and tea. An experiment with chokecherry jelly from an indigenous tree resulted in mixed reviews from the family.

Black-eyed Susans, daisies, a daisylike yellow flower, pinks, thyme and yellow and white sedums do well in the thin soil and withstand the wind. Yet the combination of wind, hot rocks and shallow soil does call for watering in dry spells. The island is not connected to electricity, so the Taits installed a gasoline-driven motor to pump water up to a tank on a tower. The tower has become a thing of beauty in itself. In a handmade wooden box, Jim starts morning glory seeds, encouraging germination by soaking and cracking the seeds. When the shoots send up tendrils, he moves the box to the base of the tower. By August, blue morning glories wind up 12 feet (3.6 m) of latticework, giving a glorious vertical element to the garden.

Jim may have inherited interest in gardening from his great-grandfather, a garden designer who emigrated from Scotland and designed many of the gardens in Fredericton. Later he moved to Charlottetown, where he was a florist. James Senior laid out some of the parks in the capital of Prince Edward Island. Jim's grandmother, Martha Boone, was the first to garden on Empress Island, starting in the 1940s.

The Tait and Boone families prefer to maintain most of their 26 acres (10.5 ha) in its natural state, with junipers, pines, oaks and ferns. Despite use of the property by four generations, in June, a stone's throw from the cottage, bunchberry, starflower, false Solomon's seal and half a dozen substantial clumps of pink lady's slipper bloom in shady places. Indeed Jim is so loathe to disturb a tree that when they were expanding a sleeping cabin into their present comfortable cottage, they made the bedrooms extremely narrow rather than cut down a magnificent pine, though Adrienne sometimes wonders about the decision while trying to make the beds.

In 1975 a severe storm blew down a huge white pine near the cottage. Jim planted a young pine in the same spot and it's now more than 15 feet (4.5 m) tall. In a boggy spot, he introduced several eastern larch; these have feathery pale green needles that turn to gold in the autumn and fall off. He has also planted an ash and trembling aspen.

Although numerous blueberry patches dot the island, the Taits never know from one year to the next whether the bushes will produce berries. Much depends on the rainfall at the time the bushes set flowers and fruit. The Taits water some blueberry patches, a practice that may have proven inviting to an unexpected visitor. One dry summer, Adrienne was indoors when she was startled to see a hairy arm reaching up on the porch to one of the hanging baskets of flowers. The explorer was a black bear, likely visiting the island in search of blueberries, which were sparse on the mainland that year. The bear ambled away from the cottage, swam to an adjacent island and clambered gracefully ashore, where it found a fish head and sat on a rock for a leisurely picnic.

Apart from the cottages, the outer islands off Pointe-au-Baril, with their wind-sculpted pines, smooth rounded rocks and blueberry patches probably look much the same today as they did when Samuel de Champlain paddled past on his voyage of 1615 en route to Huronia.

At windy Empress Island, morning glories, seeded in a handmade box in a sheltered spot, twine toward the water tower.

❧ STONE WALL PROTECTS PERENNIALS ❧

The Hertzberg gardens on Lake Joseph are breathtaking, with 2,000 square feet (190 m²) of perennials, an innovative scree garden designed by a plantswoman, plus a pond created by a lily enthusiast.

Choosing a site for their new cottage back in 1960, the Hertzbergs couldn't resist a Yoho Island lot with water on three sides. At that point, wind wasn't a consideration. But in 1985, when Peter Hertzberg took early retirement, he wanted to spend five and a half months at the lake. In that case, said Anne Hertzberg, already an enthusiastic and knowledgeable gardener, she had to have a garden at the cottage.

The garden's greatest enemy turned out to be wind, blowing in from the southwest, west and north. It's "really sheer folly" to attempt window boxes in such windy conditions, she says. Light things may bend in a gust but heavy plants are destroyed and "you can't do anything but scream and cry."

She grows begonias, licorice plant, bidens and the trailing plants twinspur (*Diascia*) and tradescantia in boxes on the deck. She's trying a new petunia, Surfinia, which sprawls instead of straggling upward and could prove wind resistant. Sometimes she gets up in the middle of a windy night to lift the boxes to a more protected spot.

A stand of cedars provided some shelter for the first new garden, but Anne knew she would need more windbreak. So she had a 3 1/2-foot (1 m) wall built from flat native rock. The wall works well as a shelter, though it isn't quite what she planned. At the two-thirds height she had

Alpine plants used to windy conditions grow in a scree bed beside the water garden.

expected to put in soil, then another riser of stone, then more soil so that plants could be inserted. Instead the wall went up in plain rock. In the years since, the effect has been softened as naturalized sedum positions itself on the rock wall.

Anne, an active member of the Garden Club of Toronto and a founder of the new Canadian branch of the American Ivy Society, is the chief gardener in the family. Peter is the waterer and staker, so adept that her gardening friends want to clone him. As well, he looks after the grass that he wanted to plant in front of the cottage.

Peter's most visible contribution is the lily pond. In front of the cottage, he dug down to bare rock, in an area of about 30 square feet (2.7m²), about 2 feet (.6 m) below ground at the midpoint, then installed a heavy plastic liner and a filter system. Rocks for a rock garden were placed around the pond. He would have liked a couple more feet of depth to provide greater volume. A pond like his, which holds 350 gallons (about 1,500 L) of water, supports a maximum of two water lilies. He would also have preferred an outside state-of-the-art filter system, but it would have been difficult to hide.

The water lilies he likes survive winter only in deeper water where roots descend below the ice. So each fall, he removes water lilies in home-made chicken-wire cages and carries them to a cousin's boathouse, where they are sunk below the level of ice.

Anne built the pond garden up with native rock and planted cranes-

Lilies and perennials flourish behind a rock wall erected to protect plants from the wind.

bill, campanula, a fall-flowering Scotch heather (*Calluna*), moss, sedum, dicentra and grasses such as papyrus that she takes home and grows in her plant room under lights.

In the perennial gardens, watering is important not just because wind dries the plants. The original soil is so sandy that water drained right through and not even periwinkle would grow without the addition of buckets of richer soil.

In the mid-80s, Anne had two small gardens at the cottage. She had these dug up with the surrounding blueberry bushes and grasses and brought in 15 tons of soil, supplemented yearly now with fifty bags transported across the ice.

At the west end of the cottage in a partly shaded garden, Anne planted a beardtongue (*Penstemon barbuties*), astilbe, hosta, spiderwort, lady's mantle, lily of the valley, peach-leafed bellflower, phlox, daylilies, a glorious clump of lilium, a Froebel's spirea, and creeping Jenny (*Lysimachia nummularia*).

Anne cleverly disguises tree stumps with ground covers, including creeping phlox and a low blue juniper. In another area of this west garden, she planted cranesbill, meadow rue, *Oenothera*, known as sundrops, and the upward-growing *Lysimachia punctata*, as well as *Astrantia major*, a long-blooming plant, with "the strangest green flowers," that does beautifully at the cottage. Lupines, Shastas, phlox, centaurea and coreopsis also thrive here.

Bellflowers (*Campanulas*) are an excellent group of plants for the cottage, she says, as is the geranium called cranesbill, not to be confused with the common geranium (*Pelargonium*). Anne has also found beebalm or bergamot (*Monarda didyma*) a satisfactory plant in Muskoka.

Much depends on snow cover, she finds. In the winter of '95, with so little snow, she lost seven miniature roses as well as a floribunda and a huge clump of lovely Japanese anemones.

In front of the deck she prizes a blue Himalayan poppy, a plant she always wanted and which she hopes will be hardy in the Muskoka plant hardiness Zone 5.

In a shaded garden in front of the deck she has four miniature hostas, including Hosta Sugarplum, full-sized hostas, bleeding heart, astilbe, *Corydalis lutea*, a good shade plant with spurred yellow flowers, and a white-and-grey Japanese painted fern. *Astilbe chinensis*, with its small flowering spike in pink, has covered the ground from a "tiny bit" of plant and is very rewarding.

Anne says she composts "madly" and would recommend three bins for serious cottage gardeners. She sifts compost and puts it in small bags so it can be carried to the garden in the spring. Anne uses what she calls Muskoka fertilizer — 4 parts compost, 3 parts wood ash, 2 parts bonemeal, 1 part bloodmeal — mixed and thrown all over the garden gently, once things have come through in the spring.

In a sunny curved garden across the path from the deck, a continual rainbow shines from heliopsis, red Maltese cross (*Lychnis chaldedonica*), spiderwort, daylilies, chives, phlox and prairie mallow, (*Sidalcea*) with thin spires of pink flowers and the unusual attribute of two distinctive shapes of leaves.

To construct her scree garden, Hertzberg put down 6 to 8 inches (15–20 cm) of sand, then 2 to 3 inches (5–7 cm) of soil. Depending on whose advice you take, she says, this could be simply soil under each plant. A layer of pea gravel tops it up. To suit alpine plants, the soil in scree gardens must be quick-draining. "I can't recommend them more. I made a small one and doubled it in 1993."

Her scree garden plants include saxifrage, *Campanula garganica*, with bright gold-green leaves, storksbill (*Erodium x variabile* Bishop's Form), closely related to hardy geraniums, dianthus, draba — a tiny alpine plant with lemon-yellow flowers — tiny poppies, and a white rhodohypolis. She takes some of her alpine plants home to protect them during the winter.

A kidney-shaped garden in full sun is one of her favourites, bright with *Oenothera pumilla*, also known as *Oenothera perennis*, daylilies (*Hemerocallis*), painted daisies (*Pyrethrum*), tradescantia, white astilbe, and *Lilium* with primula blooming in the spring.

In addition, Anne Hertzberg, as official propogator for the ivy society, is raising about sixty ivies at the cottage. With Anne's perseverance, expertise and imagination, this wind-swept garden has become exceptional.

❧ CONSTANT WIND ❧

After his vegetable garden was well established at the family cottage on Ojibway Island, Timothy Regan vowed, no more gardens. But in 1988 he and Gail Regan built a stunning new cottage on a barren island much farther out into Georgian Bay. Wooden docks joined one tumble of rocks to another. Inspired by his favourite local example of architecture — the tower of the Ojibway Club — up soared a landmark dwelling known as "Brooker."

Brooker Island is perhaps the most exposed inhabited island off Pointe-au-Baril and an unlikely site for any kind of garden. With the constant wind, he says, the soil atop the septic bed would have been hurled at the cottage like a storm of sandpaper. So the bed had to be seeded, and soil was added well beyond the septic bed to a length of about 120 feet (40 m). He chose a deep-rooted tough turf often used on golf courses, seeded in the spring, and saw a full lawn that summer.

Soon after, he was back to gardening. With the experience gained at this island, Timothy Regan could probably garden successfully at most locations in the country, polar icecap excepted. He cut branches from a sturdy willow tree, rooted

Trial and error determined the plants that survive on this wind-whipped Georgian Bay island.

them in water and planted them as a windbreak. Wild roses grew on the island; he gave them more soil.

Along one side of the lawn, he planted lilies, sage, chamomile and peas, which he prizes for their property of fixing nitrogen in the soil. The peas were also prized by a deer that one July swam to the island and devoured the pea crop. Onions, potatoes, bush beans and radishes thrive in beds on the other side of the lawn. Near the point of the island sprawls a strawberry patch.

On Brooker Island most of the soil comes from compost. A sprinkler system distributes one-acre-inch of water a week, but when the wind is blowing the wrong way the sprinkles end up watering Georgian Bay. Timothy plans to switch to a drip system. To improve windbreak, he moved some scrub cedar and in a sheltered bed protected by the cedars he grows vegetables. A three-week drought one year when the Regans

were away took out the peppers and most of the carrots. In soil in rock crevices he grows chives, parsley, dill and mint for tea. Lettuce self seeds.

Timothy finds crops mature several weeks later on windswept Brooker Island than do those on Ojibway Island, nearer shore. Under these extremes, plants need to be tough. He envisaged an all-lily garden, but not all the specimens have proven hardy, although he has seen some of his lilies bloom into November. Wild iris are survivors, and he's now resolutely transplanting clumps of them around the various beds.

Timothy Regan says that any year he could expect to arrive and find the garden gone. In one exceptionally severe summer storm, wind lashed great waves over the island and against the windows of the cottage. A sailboat tied on the deck of the dock disappeared. Yet two days later, he was able to show that most of his plants had survived.

❧ WINDPROOF: SEDUMS AND LILYPADS ❧

When boatloads of party guests arrived at the Melhuish island on Georgian Bay, they used to be greeted by an Inukshuk — the type of stone likeness of a person that the Inuit people build to mark a trail. The winds of the 1995 July storm hurled the massive stones into the bay. That storm, etched into the history of cottaging in Ontario, isn't typical. But the winds that buffet the outer islands north of Honey Harbour in every season do determine what plants may be successfully introduced.

Duggan Melhuish and his wife, Alistair, have been cottagers at the Cognashene community off Honey Harbour all their lives. Duggan claims he knows nothing about gardening and detests related chores such as weeding. He suggests that Manitou never meant people to have manicured gardens along the eastern shores of Georgian Bay and that His plan called for white pine sprinkled into rock crevices, seagulls to drop seedlings of pin cherry, mountain ash and sumac, and naturally occurring patches of crusted lichen in greyish green or brilliant orange.

But Duggan Melhuish does like things to look well. In 1987, when the Melhuishes made their main cottage available to children and grandchildren, they built a cabin on an outer island. It's been in the family since 1939 when Duggan's father, a second-generation cottager, bought it for fifty dollars. Building regulations for the cabin required a black polypropylene pipe to transport waste along the rock to a holding tank. Something had to be done to cover up the

In a pond at a Georgian Bay cottage, a frog makes a home among the water lilies, water hyacinths and oxygenating plants.

pipe. Duggan snorkelled along the shoreline, gathering quartz, granite and black basalt to make an edging wall. Into the resulting trench he dumped some two hundred bags of soil brought from a city nursery.

At first he planted all sorts of perennials that looked attractive in garden catalogues. Time and again the wind mowed them down. Then someone suggested sedums, tough low-growing plants that withstand wind. Duggan believes he may now have the largest variety of sedums on Georgian Bay. He added Silver Mound artemisia and hen and chickens. Seeds of yarrow, loosestrife, Joe-Pye-weed and butter-and-eggs, also called toadflax, sowed themselves.

"Now, when the wild winds blow, the bushy heads of the colourful blossoms and foliage of the sedums whistle a triumph of survival as they comb the rushing westerlys through their resistant, stubby stems," Duggan Melhuish wrote in the periodical *Georgian Bay To-day*. "And the grasses whip about, bending and swaying yet managing to retain their dignity and an upright position when the storm is past."

Duggan next built a second rock garden, heaving large rocks to enclose it in the shade on the south side of the cottage and around below the deck. Ferns and hosta established the background with dahlias and astilbe in the foreground. Mosses and impatiens form a border.

In the fourth year of gardening, he launched a small lily pond with a "wee" fountain that splashes water onto a slab of granite. The pond contains a yellow pond lily (*Nuphar variegatum Engelm*) and a fragrant white water lily (*Nymphaea odorata Ait*). He added arrowhead (*Sagittaria latifolia*), pickerel weed (*Pontederia cordata*) and duckweed (*Lemna minor*) for the smallmouth bass to nibble. The pond is surrounded with yellow and blue pansies, Austrian and white pine, cedar, daisies, potentilla and artemisia. A wooden rudder, painted blue and white, tells time by the sun.

Finally, he constructed a big, 30-by-8–foot (9 by 2.4 m) pond at the south end of the island in a rocky hollow. The first step was to hire a man with a machine to dig out the boulders, accumulated grasses and scrub. When "the glorious day arrived" to fill the cleared basin with water from the firehose, the Melhuishes watched with dismay as all the water in the pond drained out through faults in the rock into Georgian Bay. A stonemason was called in to rescue the project with cement and flagstones of pink granite from Parry Sound.

An extensive collection of yellow, pink and white lilies was planted in whisky tubs set 1 1/2 feet (45 cm) below the surface. Duggan chose Moore, Pink Sensation, Comanche and the native bullhead lily (*Nuphar variegatum*) and added water hyacinths (*Eichhornia crassipes*) and oxygenating plants. Pickerel weed and arrowhead established themselves. Wild iris and cardinal flower (*Lobelia cardinalis*) grow nearby.

After seagulls gobbled the golden fantails swimming in the pond, Duggan put in smallmouth bass, which add to the effect and can also be panfried for guests. Bullfrogs moved into the pond to sun themselves on the water lilies.

Duggan Melhuish likes to take his coffee down to the pond early in a summer morning and watch the reflection of the sun rising. Then about nine A.M., the lilies, closed into cones for the night, start spreading their petals as if opening their faces to the sun. At times, he reflects on the eyesore that started him gardening — that four-inch pipe.

Sedums cling to the rocks
at an island where wind sculpts the conifers.

The fieldstone wall of a cottage at Lake of Bays helps create a microclimate for the perennial border.

❧ MICROCLIMATE FOR A BORDER ❧

As a visitor rounds a bend in the lane, the cottage comes into view like an illustration from a book of fairy tales, a stone dwelling with a border of flowers serene in the summer sun. Barbara Hill purposely created an English-style border to complement the century-old fieldstone of the cottage, which has been in her husband's family for more than fifty years.

Contrasted with all the challenges presented by most gardens on the Precambrian Shield, conditions at this garden on Lake of Bays seem almost magical. The border never suffers from winterkill, isn't disturbed by animals, and hasn't required

rock excavations. It grows profusely from the enrichment of compost without commercial soil mixtures or fertilizers. Best of all, it's protected from wind summer and winter by the back wall of the cottage. The main challenge is keeping it watered.

Not incidentally, Barbara Hill is a senior adviser in the horticulture section of the Garden Club of Toronto and she characteristically perseveres with plants. But she is the first to say that her splendid English border occupies an "ideal spot."

She has encouraged a long season of bloom. English daisies appear early among Johnny jump-ups. Clematis, delphiniums, lilies and miniature roses flowered cooperatively during a July family reunion. In August, pink, red and burgundy beebalm, phlox and fringed bleeding heart bloom with a hybrid tea rose and an unusual yellow lacy-leafed chrysanthemum. Moonbeam coreopsis and a black-eyed Susan shine into September.

In the border, she established cranesbill geraniums, *Sedum spectabile*, gloriosa daisies, lady's mantle and euphorbia. Barbara is aware of the controversy over purple loosestrife invading wetlands in Canada, but she assures visitors a specimen of *Lythrum* Morden Mink, grown for twenty years in her garden, has not spread.

At one end of the border, a corrugated wooden box, like an old cigar box, hooks onto a stake. Designed to trap earwigs, the box can be dumped into a pail of hot water.

Among her favourite plants are the daisylike helenium, a light blue scented geranium, and a white-blooming Popcorn mini-rose. The dahlias she grows herself. A rose-coloured nasturtium comes from seed that she says, without revealing the source, is hard to find. Herbs include oregano, feverfew, golden rue and chives. Along the shaded west side of the cottage, she plants Blitz impatiens among hosta against the wall, which lights up as the sun sets.

Her container plantings reflect her experience. She won a prize in the city for a gigantic coleus that spills out of a container placed near the front verandah beside an old bell from a locomotive. An antique fire basket from the Moffat stove firm makes another unusual planter. A yellow container on a natural wicker stand holds an arrangement of ivy, black-eyed Susan and white pine.

Barbara likes to try different plants. By the dock, a container holds *Scaevola aemula*, a blue-flowered trailing plant that originated in Tasmania, licorice plant (*Helichrysum petiolatum*), a native of South Africa with trailing grey foliage, and *Pelargonium graveolas* Grey Lady Plymouth.

She prefers to keep the lakeside of the cottage in a more natural setting, though a row of Balm of Gilead trees planted by a previous owner makes an unusual sight for Muskoka. In spring it smells like orange blossoms. "We're an active family, with waterskiing, windsurfing and boating. I don't want to take away from the natural look at the front."

The dock from which the Hills pursue their summer sports sits on a crib fashioned with square-headed nails. It's more than a hundred years old. It was part of a logging operation that took place a century ago at this site on Trading Bay. A lumbering firm called Gilmour and Co. obtained the rights to log white pine in Algonquin Park. They floated the logs down the Oxtongue River and into Lake of Bays to Trading Bay, where they built a mile-long sluiceway to take the logs up over the height of land. To pump the water to float the logs up, they constructed a power station o the original stone building that is now the Hills' cottage. After acquiring the building in the '40s, the Hill family began a meticulous collection of memorabilia from the logging years.

Come the end of October, Barbara rakes leaves, cuts back the garden plants, and covers the gardens with evergreen boughs, pines or cedar. She also hills up the roses. "I have intense winter sun, so often snow melts against the stone. Because of the house, rains don't often beat in at the back. I compost and I have enough to put on my gardens every year. I don't add commercial manure, but some peat and limestone. I put it on when I work the gardens in the spring."

Lest the garden sound surreally problem free, Barbara Hill notes ruefully, "My big work is planting in the spring with the mosquitoes and black-flies."

❦ STAKING AN EXPANDING GARDEN ❦

You can hear the drone of bees as soon as you come within sight of the lush hillside garden at the tip of Acton Island. Pink, red and purple bergamot — aptly called beebalm — quivers as swarms of bees sip nectar. A woodchip path curves through the garden past more than sixty types of perennials down to the cottage overlooking Lake Muskoka.

Mike Edgecombe is partial to tall plants — hollyhocks, delphiniums, lilies, and inula, a sunflower-like plant that in his garden reaches 7 feet (2 m), purple coneflower and heliopsis. Although he has tried to place gardens where they are not exposed to the wind, a northeast storm sweeps in at an angle to the hillside. So he does "a lot of staking," using bamboo poles for the hollyhocks. Delphiniums he finds so brittle that they snap, so he is planning to move them to a more sheltered spot.

On windy days the garden dries out fast. The sprinkler system is arranged with heads high up on pipes so that usually water runs down the surface to beds below, but on windy days the spray blows in the wrong direction. He has also tried a sprinkler system in the flower boxes, but has returned to manual watering, fertilizing once a week.

The hillside garden, partly under a maple, is edged with green and white euonymus and a carpet juniper. A clump of white iris that grows more than 5 feet (1.5 m) tall punctuates the garden in late spring, followed by lupines.

Come summer the scent of lilies is almost intoxicating. Gloriosa daisies, obedient plant, goatsbeard, disc bell hibiscus, agastache, heliopsis, *Anchusa azurea*, astilbe, phlox and a great clump of Chinese lanterns bloom with monkshood, liatris, purple loosestrife, Jacob's ladder and polyantha Fairy rose. He recently planted six Explorer roses, which he planned to take out and bury in the soil as an alternative to hilling around them for the winter.

Barbara and Michael Edgecombe purchased their first cottage on Acton Island in 1970 and in 1987 made it available to their four children, building a new summer home on an adjoining lot. Mike says his father was English and maintained a rock garden in the city, but as a youth, his own involvement was limited to cutting the grass. While he later did some gardening at a city home, his interest zoomed when he came to the cottage. He finds gardening gets his mind off everything as he relaxes up north. "I love puttering and gardening to the point where I have created a monster. . . . One bed led to another."

He started with the hillside garden, hiring a landscaper to do the heavy work. Every summer he thinks, "Maybe this would look better over there," and creates new beds, bringing in topsoil by the truckload. One bed on the northwest side of the cottage functions as a nursery where he tries out plants before transplanting.

In front of the cottage he used a heavy pressure hose to clear off the grass and wild strawberries, exposing stratified bedrock. Mike admires the exposed rock: "To me, that's Muskoka." On the rock by the flagpole he planted lilies, turtlehead, beebalm and sedums, including *Sedum telephium* Autumn Joy. On the other side of the boathouse flowers glow — zinnias from one bed, dahlias from another, with coneflowers, phlox, yellow lilies and snapdragons. Most beds on the rock are filled with perennials, but one holds impatiens, begonias, and for cutting, cosmos and snapdragons. A blue spruce, copper maple and pale green globe cedar rise from the rock to meet the deck at the cottage.

On the boathouse, along decks and by the gazebo, flower boxes are filled with cascading geraniums in fire-engine red and salmon shades. He adds a pellet of fertilizer that's supposed to last forty-five days, but tops that up with more.

Mike has also experimented with plants he admires in Florida, including pink mandeville, which he digs out of the garden like an annual at the end of the season and stores at a local nursery. In a twist on the traditional garden journal, he's working with a computer program to map the garden layout and keep track of "what is where."

In summer, Mike says, he toils at least a couple of hours daily in the garden, while in the spring he will work solidly in bursts of two or three days at a time. Student Sean Marshall of Yellowknife worked full-time in the garden during several summers and "without him I'd be lost," Mike says, particularly as a longtime back problem has flared up again.

It was Sean who suggested cutting bars of Irish Spring soap in quarters and putting them on stakes to discourage deer. The tactic is still in the early stages, but so far deer have not returned to damage the garden. Chipmunks "love Iceland poppies for some reason" and chew on daisies and sunflowers, but Mike leaves them alone and has taken the sunflowers out of the garden.

Mike Edgecombe enjoys cutting flowers and arranging them, often spending an hour or so to achieve the effect he wants. "You have to have enough in there; it's like planting annuals close together so they're very bushy." He says he must be making progress because his wife no longer rearranges them.

Trailing geraniums sway with the breeze in flower boxes at Acton Island.

Hosta in bloom benefits from a watering system that keeps soil moist in a dry, windswept garden on Royal Muskoka Island.

❦ WATER SYSTEM DEFEATS WIND ❦

The average cottage pump couldn't maintain enough pressure to water the garden at one cottage perched high up on Royal Muskoka Island.

A prevailing east wind and stormy northwest winds dry the soil and desiccate the plants. And as an added factor, water must be pumped up 80 feet (24 m) from Lake Rosseau to the level of the cottage and then along 150 feet (45 m) to the start of a border that curves around the length and far width of the septic bed. "It's so hot and breezy up here, it dries out really fast," says Susan Biggar. "When I was using a garden hose sprinkler I would have to leave it on for two hours at each end of the garden."

Her solution is a drip irrigation system set on a timer. It comes on three times a day for two hours at a time. The timer ensures that the soil stays moist even if the family has to be away from the cottage for a week. And, of course, the system can be turned off during rainy periods.

Susan says it's easy to install. She put the hoses in the 200-foot (60 m) garden herself. Although they're on the surface, they're largely hidden by the tall perennials she planted. In the fall she disconnects the system, drains the hoses and brings them in. The system gives a kick-start to the gardening season by providing moisture in June when the family may be kept in the city by end-of-school activities.

Royal Muskoka Island was the site of the Royal Muskoka Hotel and home for many years to the Muskoka Lakes Association Regatta. After the hotel burned down in 1952, the shoreline was divided into ninety cottage lots and the remaining lands left as beautiful cut meadows. Come July, you can still see orange daylilies lining the roadside near the old entrance to the hotel.

Jim and Susan Biggar bought two lots. They used to climb to the highest elevation for picnics and decided to construct their cottage at that site in 1971. Except for a shade garden of astilbe, coral bells, hosta and impatiens abutting the cottage, the septic bed garden, and the removal of some trees to give a view of the lake, the Biggars have left their property in its natural forested state. Their cottage appears to float in a tree canopy of mature hemlock and pine. Lichens and blueberry bushes cover the rocks on the lakeside, and in the rich woods chanterelle mushrooms grow beside a mossy log.

The family worked together building a low rock wall that outlines the main perennial garden, edging the septic bed. They used some rocks from the property and purchased others in Parry Sound. At its widest, the garden reaches about 3 feet (1 m). They laid a landscape cloth down first, then sand, then filled in to a depth of about 1 1/2 feet (45 cm) with soil mixed with peat moss, which they moved in by wheelbarrow.

At the far end of the garden, which can be seen from the kitchen window, Susan enjoys a spring show of lily of the valley, violets and forget-me-nots, set off later with pink impatiens, blue iris and the purple of the wild plant heal-all.

Susan, a member of the Garden Club of Hamilton, recalls the fun of choosing perennials to fill the long garden. "I couldn't walk by a store without saying, 'I'll have one of those.'" Among the perennials set in repeating drifts are lady's mantle, lavatera, with its delicate pink bells, fragrant globe thistles, black-eyed Susans, purple coneflowers, purple beebalm or bergamot, the purple spires of liatris, yarrow, phlox, hosta and Johnny jump-ups. At the front, ajuga provides a low ground cover, and one summer she planted an edible addition, leafy radicchio.

Susan recently placed several clumps of Queen Anne's lace at the rear of the border. Swaths of Asiatic lilies in red, white, peach, yellow and gold scattered about the garden provide bloom for weeks during mid- to late summer. In the summer of '96, despite cooler weather and plenty of cloud in July, Susan found her plants grew taller than ever. She stakes them unobtrusively as protection from the ever-present wind with twigs, sticks and twine. A huge white purple-martin bird-house, which her husband constructed from an illustration and roofed with 1,600 tiny dollhouse shingles, glued on by hand, has become a striking garden ornament.

Despite the wind and heat at that elevation, Susan Biggar has created what must be one of the prettiest gardens on a septic bed at any cottage.

❧ FINDING WHAT WORKS ❧

The great fun in gardening at the cottage, says Chris Hughes, is in seeing what will survive. Starting with wonderful visions, you experiment to discover plants that will withstand the climate and soil, try again and end up with "the odd success" that makes it all worthwhile.

Her stunning sunny gardens on Kindersley Island in the Cognashene community of islands in Georgian Bay off Honey Harbour owe much to knowledgeable experimentation. Chris Hughes gardened at homes in Montreal and Toronto and says she has been inspired by membership in the Garden Club of Toronto, where she shares experiences with enthusiastic gardeners and takes useful courses.

At her cottage, she notes, wind is probably the most damaging factor, with the prevailing wind from the west, as well as blows from the north. By trial and error, backed up by her considerable practical experience, she has identified a wide range of shrubs and plants that withstand the wind on the exposed rocky slope between the cottage and Georgian Bay. Behind the boathouse, she took advantage of created and natural shelters to build a garden that embraces roses and perennials. And behind the cottage, her daughter nurtures a substantial vegetable garden.

Many of the basic beds were in place in front of the cottage when the Hughes bought the property in the mid-80s, and existing coniferous shrubs including mugho pine and juniper provided some windbreak.

Chris finds that nothing bothers tall sedum and lilies survive just about any wind. Asiatic lilies are available in varieties that bloom successively throughout July and August. "I try all sorts of things. Lilies are wonderful, especially Asiatics and hemerocallis (daylilies), yarrow, veronicas, liatris, coreopsis, evening primrose, cinquefoil potentilla, weigela, Northern Gold forsythia, spirea."

Around a flagpole, she planted ground covers such as ajuga, sedum, thrift and creeping Jenny. And behind the flagpole in a spot with little soil, she placed sedum, thyme and ajuga with wild iris and cranesbill geranium. A garden below the flagpole brims over with liatris, phlox, zinnias, cosmos, iris, yarrow, lilies, blue and white veronica, nicotiana, perennial geranium, monarda or beebalm, pinks and lavender.

Her husband, Paul, constructed a tiered lily-pond where frogs promptly made a home. An unusual white creeping mother-of-thyme grows nearby. Beyond the lily pond toward the lake, a common lilac flourishes, and nearer the house she has found Prestonii lilacs hardy. In one crevice she planted lilies, potentilla, weigela, Anthony Waterer spirea, mother-of-thyme, snow-in-summer, Pink Panda strawberries and campanula.

She finds some plants winter better at the cottage than in Toronto because the crevices in rock catch the snow and protect it from the freeze-thaw-freeze cycle that is so damaging. In the winter of '94–95, noted for its lack of snow, she lost a number of plants, including eight roses. The Hughes leave the cottage too early to cover the roses, but shrub roses and Explorer roses don't need to be covered, she says. The hardy shrub hybrid rose, Thérèse Bugnet, originally bred in Alberta, was an exception, surviving that winter, as did her Explorer roses, bred in Ottawa and later at L'Assomption, Quebec, for exceptional hardiness. Such roses are a boon for cottagers who are away after freeze-up.

Containers flank the steps leading down from the porch and junipers anchor the crest of the rock. An outdoor hot tub with petunias at the four corners provides a perfect spot for stargazing. Past that, the front garden ends with a blue heron sculpted by Paul Hughes of driftwood and bleached branches. A stone wall that he reduced in height for aesthetics provides windbreak for a path leading to the dock and boathouse. On the other side of the path, potentilla and cedar hedges provide more shelter.

Chris has several goals for her garden. She believes a cottage garden should not be formal and she aims for a succession of bloom. When the cottage is opened in the third week of April, daffodils and other bulbs are coming up in the woods; the obedient plant (*Physostegia*) is one of the plants that comes into bloom in August.

At the end of the boathouse, sheltered from wind by a native elderberry pruned to an attractive shape, Chris grows roses. Among them are William Baffin, her favourite of the Explorer roses, John Cabot, a fragrant mauve-red Canadian climber particularly suited to the severe winter, Jens Munk, and a Friendship rose from Holland. She is also trying a Henry Kelsey rose recommended by the Royal Botanical Gardens.

Hollyhocks, morning glory, sweetpeas, cleome, creeping phlox and love-in-a-mist (*Nigella damascena*), an annual that has reseeded, make a sweet, old-fashioned picture. Yellow corydalis, a gift from her friend Anne Hertzberg, grows with astilbe, yarrow and a columbine, partly eaten by "some nasty grub."

Behind the cottage sits a garden that's a symbolic treasure to Chris — her daughter's raised vegetable patch. "I'm so thrilled she's into gardening." Cindy started gardening around 1993 and each year expands her range. Paul built a frame of logs and rocks, and the family brought in soil to start her off. The garden boasts Early Girl tomatoes, cherry tomatoes, bush beans, carrots and snow peas. A white cosmos has spread in an amazingly vigorous clump and a beautiful wood sorrel (*Oxalis inopsis*) rests in one corner. Herb enthusiast Chris squeezes in parsley, sage, oregano and other favourites around the edges of her daughter's garden.

Meanwhile, her experiments continue. One of her latest is mallow (*Lavatera trimestris*), a bushy plant with hollyhock-like flowers that blooms from mid to late summer and does best in full sun and average soil. Usually considered an annual, it will reseed. In time it may be added to the successes of this prolific garden in Georgian Bay.

Asiatic lilies survive just about any wind and, with Oriental lilies, contribute colour all summer.

Native Plants

Encouraging or establishing native plants at the cottage calls for good powers of observation. What plants are already growing? What is the natural habitat of the plants you want to transplant, buy or grow from seed? Are they situated in shade, sun, open spaces, understorey woodland, boggy spots, a post-burn site, cracks in the rocks? Are they at home in deep or shallow soil, sand or acidic peat? Which ones attract birds or butterflies?

Cottagers making their second homes in a relatively untouched area will want to move with caution lest they destroy the natural habitat they found so enticing in the first place. Those buying or inheriting a cottage may find that construction and foot traffic from previous owners have eliminated many indigenous plants. Those that remain can be encouraged, and it may be possible to reintroduce some species.

As in any other endeavour, appreciation increases with knowledge. Knowing the name of that small leathery-leafed plant with the white berries or that fall-blooming aster can open the mind to the world of indigenous plants. One gardener in this book had been seeing ferns at her cottage for a quarter of century, but never really looked at them until a relative identified a maidenhair fern. Soon she was strolling about the property, observing the differences in the ferns, reading about and

ABOVE: *Wild grasses are integral to a prairie garden at Stony Lake.*
AT LEFT: *Yellow lady's slipper shines in a woodland garden featuring native plants.*

studying them. Her neighbours now beg her to share her knowledge.

Some cottagers prefer to enjoy the pines, maples, birches, juniper and leaf litter of the forest in its natural state without introducing any other plants. But for those who want to garden, Glen Lumas, professor of landscape horticulture at the University of Guelph, suggests that introduced plants be maintained in a "horticultural envelope" around the cottage. As you move further from manmade structures to bush or open area, it would seem appropriate to reduce, then eliminate plants that are not indigenous, moving from the cultivated to the wild.

Lumas and his colleagues, Carol Ann Lacroix and Henry Kock, caution that certain plants should not be introduced into properties on the Canadian Shield. Vinca (periwinkle), goutweed, Boston ivy, Norway maple, dame's rocket and a cultivar of native bittersweet compete too vigorously with plants in the wild. Also, the strong smell of nicotiana will obscure delectable natural fragrances.

If you see a native plant you would like for the cottage, don't steal it from the wild, Lumas advises. If the plant is on your property and you want to move it to where it will be better seen, you would need to take as much of its surroundings as could be moved by a backhoe and bucket unless it is moving to a site with precisely the same conditions as its original location. Look at the slope of the land and the community of plants that grows with the one you want. Try to relocate it to a similar community and site. Also before transplanting a native plant, you should make sure the population is large enough to sustain the loss.

When buying native plants from garden centres, it is appropriate to ask where the plants came from, to ensure that you are not encouraging companies that poach from the wild. A label of "nursery grown" may mean the plant has merely been tended at the nursery. Look for plants that are "nursery propogated." Several companies in Muskoka propogate native plants for sale.

Be particularly cautious with the following species, which are being grown by few nurseries at this time: bloodroot (*Sanguinaria canadensis*), bottle gentian (*Gentiana andrewsii*), Dutchman's breeches (*Dicentra cucullaria*), hepatica (*Hepatica americana, H. acutiloba*), Jack-in-the-pulpit (*Arisaema atrorubens or A. triphyllum*), large-flowered bellwort (*Uvularia grandiflora*), pitcher plant (*Sarracenia purpurea*), all species of orchids and trilliums, and trout-lily or dog-toothed violet (*Erythronium americanum*). These are among the most difficult wildflowers to grow from seed, but seeds can be purchased by catalogue or obtained in the seed exchange of the Canadian Wildflower Society.

To grow a native plant from seed from a plant in the wild, Henry Kock advises, note its location in your garden journal, and return when the seed ripens. Place the seed in an envelope. Try to figure out how it is normally dispersed. Small seeds can usually be scattered on the surface of a pot. If it had a cover, then bury it. If it is a fleshy fruit that would normally be eaten by birds, you may have to add sulphuric acid or plant it in a peaty soil. Plant in a clay pot, label it, mulch with leaves or grass, cover with fine wire mesh to discourage mice and deer, and put the pot partway down in soil or wood shavings for the winter.

Carol Ann Lacroix, president of the Dogtooth Chapter of the Canadian Wildflower Society, says native plants require less maintenance than introduced species. Native plants in their proper sites do not require as much soil preparation or soil additives such as fertilizer. She also finds that wildflower gardens require less weeding. Although it hasn't been scientifically proven that native plants are more resistant to pests, wildflower enthusiasts often develop a different attitude, feeling easy, say, about a caterpillar eating butterfly weeds. Native plants have coevolved with local mammals, insects and birds, and the presence of these plants will encourage native fauna.

❧ Prairie and Woodland ❧

Jim French had always liked gardening, but acquiring a cottage in 1981 kindled a passion for wildflowers. Intrigued by a few wildflowers seen on rambles around his 2-acre property at Stony Lake in the Kawarthas, he began to visit nurseries and read about woodland flowers. Today, between a granite rock face and the east wall of the cottage, a long garden with a rich diversity of woodland flowers and ferns blooms continuously from the first hepatica of April till the finale of the large and small yellow lady's-slipper orchids early in June.

Having created that garden from "a mass of brambles, briars and brush," Jim found he had nothing to look at for the rest of the summer. So in the mid-80s he set to work on a prairie garden on the one sunny spot available — an abandoned roadway. To cover the gravel and macadam, he brought in topsoil. He tried scattering seed on the open ground, but weeds and aliens, plants such as ox-eye daisy and vetch introduced from other countries, reappeared to strangle the seedlings. Then he divided the area into small plots, digging up the aliens and putting in "a few good things" each summer. Many of them he grew from seed in special planting beds nearer the cottage, where he also sows woodland wildflower seeds.

Today the prairie garden is almost filled in. One wild blue lupine, for example, has spread to fourteen. From June to September, sun-loving wildflowers attract butterflies, bees and hummingbirds.

Along the way, Jim proposed a get-together of wildflower enthusiasts that blossomed into the Canadian Wildflower Society, which has several branches in Canada, publishes the magazine *Wildflower*, and operates a seed exchange. Jim French is the society's honorary president.

To bring wildflowers to the cottage, he transplanted some from land destined for a housing development, took others with permission from a woodlot, obtained seed from the society's exchange and collected seeds himself.

Growing native wildflowers from seed is a far trickier process than planting, say, a squash seed. Trilliums and wild blue indigo, for example, take five years or more to come into bloom. Many reproductive processes are either not known or not written about in the many wildflower books in Jim's collection. Jim says he had poor results seeding in open grounds. To assure germination, he resigned himself in some cases to sowing in pots, leaving them outside one winter to stratify, then bringing the seedlings indoors under lights. As a general rule, he says, wildflower mixes are useless. The packagers know that people like instant growth and colour so they include lots of annuals that disappear after the first year.

Jim describes himself as a "real novice" at gardening in the early '80s, but today his interests embrace grasses and sedges, ferns, native flowering trees and vines as well as the prairie and spring woodland. In the woodland, he found the sensitive fern easy to grow and also has examples of Christmas, marginal, maidenhair, interrupted, cinnamon, royal, oak and hart's tongue ferns.

He adds peat to the soil in the shady woodland garden, which includes false Solomon's seal, penstemons, white creeping bunchberry, white violets, bloodroot, Arctic iris,

Virginia bluebells, yellow lady's slipper, painted trilliums, Dutchman's breeches, lower left, and starflower, lower right, illuminate the spring season.

Virginia waterleaf, wild geranium, baneberry, white and red trilliums, Dutchman's breeches, bearberry, wood poppies, bergamot, Jack-in-the-pulpit and the related green dragon (*Arisaema dracontium*).

Jim points out that bloodroot seeds are often dispersed by ants, which take the seed underground, and at no harm to the seed, dine on a small sac on the seed, an eliasome, containing sweet nutritious juices, then transfer it to an underground garbage heap where conditions are ideal for germination.

Nearby grow summer meadow rue (*Dicentra eximia*), the dainty later-blooming native bleeding heart, wild clematis, which is growing more slowly than Jim expected, starflowers, globeflower, carrion flower, shooting star and wild roses.

Jim says animals haven't been a bother; he's content to let beaver harvest some shoreline trees and is mildly curious about "something" that munched off the tops of the showy lady's-slipper orchid one year. Frost is not a concern either. Stony Lake keeps the first frost at bay until late September or even mid-October.

The sunny prairie garden, with its soil reverting to gravel in some places, is an entirely different habitat. The flowers, grasses and sedges stand on taller stalks. Bees drone and butterflies linger on their favourite plants. You feel the sun on the back of your neck.

The prairie boasts a brilliant palette — great blue lobelia, black-eyed Susan, purple coneflowers, the orange of butterfly weed, and bottle gentian, looking like purple Christmas tree lights.

Jim is fond of penstemons, including *Penstemon smallii*, with mauve and white flowers, *Penstemon hirsutus* and *Penstemon digitalis* (white beardtongue). And he's always on the lookout for the fifteen to twenty wild grasses he planted, including Canada wild rye, bluejoint grass, big blue stem and little blue stem. Bottle gentian, blue iris, dotted blazing star, tall coreopsis, heliopsis, fairy candles and cardinal flower tower above blue-eyed grass (*Sisyrinchium montanum*), with its grasslike leaves and tiny blue flowers that bloom for only a day. Here and there in the prairie stands the sturdy cup plant, with leaves encircling the stem like a cup, catching rainwater and providing a home for small insects and larvae.

It's a challenge now to ensure that plants blooming at the same time are situated together. In mid-June, for example, wild blue lupines of the north flower at the same time as golden alexanders and prairie smoke, with its pale pink flowers that evolve into feathery seedheads. An informal path winds through the prairie. Near it on a course where water drains, Jim added Queen of the Prairie, ironweed and Joe-Pye-weed, a damp-loving perennial with scented flower-heads that bloom in late summer and are attractive to bees.

Several maples provide shade near one end of the prairie, and Jim used to rest there while struggling to get the garden established. Eventually he decided to make that spot another woodland garden with ferns, bearberry, baneberry, bunch-berry, May apple, trilliums, starflower and yellow lady-slipper. With a metal bell wind chime tinkling in the breeze, it's a peaceful oasis in which to observe the prairie garden and consider its predecessors.

Catharine Parr Traill described a prairie garden at nearby Rice Lake in pioneer days, and many prairie remnants survive in Ontario today, largely in the southwest. Prairie gardening is great fun, Jim French says. For cottagers who are enthused about wildflowers and have a sunny lot, a prairie garden is a natural alternative.

❧ SUDDENLY SEEING FERNS ❧

For many cottagers, ferns are, well, just there, in the woods and clearings, pleasant, taken for granted. Aileen Coates had enjoyed her cottage in Haliburton for twenty-five years, seeing ferns but never really looking at them, until the day when her husband Keith's mother, Audrey, showed her a clump of delicate-looking maidenhair ferns.

They were growing under an Ontario Hydro line. Concerned they might be damaged by spraying or tree felling, Aileen transplanted a small clump to nearer her cottage, where it thrived.

That summer on the same paths where she had walked hundreds of times, Aileen began noticing the ferns, realizing they were not all the same. Fronds grew in different shapes, sizes and shades. The leaflets, called pinnae, might be "cut" once or even twice. At Christmas she received a book about ferns and learned what an ancient, complicated plant form they are. Their two-generational reproduction proved fascinating. The leafy fern plant bears spores, which fall on the soil, germinate and produce a green heart-shaped prothallus, bearing the sex organs. After fertilization, the egg starts a new plant. In some plants the sterile and fertile fronds are different in appearance. And some ferns reproduce vegetatively from underground rhizomes.

By the mid-90s, on a walk around the property, Aileen could identify nineteen different ferns, many indigenous to the property, a few transplanted and a few purchased from nurseries. To her surprise, she has evolved into a collector.

In 1973, excavation for an addition to

Maidenhair fern stores its spores in the folded edges of the fronds. This one flourishes in a Haliburton garden of native plants.

the cottage on South Kashawigamog Lake resulted in an unsightly bank of earth behind the cottage. In the belief that when God gives you lemons, you make lemonade, she started a hillside garden of native plants.

Aileen says she had never gardened and is just learning. After retirement, she took botany courses at Erindale College, the University of Toronto campus in Mississauga, and joined field trips with naturalists' groups, learning what conditions favour different ferns and how to recognize one from another.

On the hillside, to the left of a path leading from the cottage, she planted a broad-leafed sensitive fern (*Onoclea sensibilis*), which has fronds that go black at the earliest frost. Near it rises an ostrich fern (*Matteuccia struthiopteris pensylvanica*), the tall fern much beloved by city gardeners. Its fiddleheads are safe to eat as a vegetable. After a groundhog trampled this specimen, Aileen removed the bottom from a plastic pot and pulled it over the plant down to the ground as a support.

She points out the interrupted fern (*Osmunda claytoniana*), which grows even bigger than the ostrich fern, and when mature will grow spores in the middle of the frond. The spore-bearing leaflets shrivel, interrupting the appearance. The nearby maidenhair fern (*Adiantum pedatum*) stores its spores neatly tucked up in folded-over edges. In the same area grows an oak fern (*Gymnocarpium dryopteris*), with its lime- to yellow-green fronds, favouring just the sort of shaded slope to which Aileen has moved it, and a Christmas fern, purchased at a nursery and probably a cultivar. She demonstrates that the lady fern

Cottagers may be surprised at the diversity of ferns on their properties; these are found at Lake Kashawigamog.

(*Athyrium filix-femina*), which produces fronds as long as 6 1/2 feet (2 m), can be distinguished by black hairs or scales on its "legs." The lacy *Dryopteris intermedia*, an evergreen wood fern, has brown scales on its stems.

Interspersed among the ferns, indigenous plants such as Canada Mayflower, starflower, wild honeysuckle, trilliums and Jack-in-the-pulpit flourish. To the right of the path, she planted a blue-green marginal shield fern (*Dryopteris marginalis*). Its spores form in dots along the margins of the pinnae. Farther along is a wild Christmas fern (*Polystichum acrostichoides*) with spores on the tips of the pinnae, which are shaped like little ears.

From a bank where a road was slated to go through, Aileen rescued a long beech fern (*Phegopteris connectilis*), which can be distinguished by pinnae shaped like a V at the bottom. Not far away is another dryopteris, the spinulose wood fern (*D. cartusiana*) with the pinnule closest to the stem the longest.

Aileen purchased one of the rarer ferns, the hart's tongue, (*Phillitis scolopendrium*) from a nursery. Its spores form straight lines on the underside. Native to the Bruce Peninsula, this fern requires alkaline soil, and so she gives it gardener's lime.

In the hillside garden, Aileen planted wild sarsaparilla, the yellow large-flowered bellwort, which looks as if the stem grows through the leaf, wild strawberries, Solomon's seal, orange and yellow hawkweed, white baneberry, heal-all, foamflower and herb Robert.

Farther back in the woods in a shady wet spot, Aileen has placed a New York fern (*Thelypteris noveboracensis*) and a royal fern (*Osmunda regalis spectabilis*), which grows in swamps, low woods and cedar bogs.

Little *Polypodium virginianum* grows best on mossy rocks. The sixteenth fern on a walk through the property is fragile fern (*Cystopteris fragilis*), usually found on cliffs or rotted logs.

On the lakeshore below the cottage during a canoe ride, Aileen and Keith Coates were thrilled to discover a beautiful specimen of cinnamon fern (*Osmunda cinnamomea*), with wonderful woolly cinnamon-coloured fertile fronds that wither after the spore are cast. Its presence means she now has examples of all three of the Osmunda ferns that grow in Canada.

Of course, the property also has its share of bracken, the coarse-fronded *Pteridium aquilinum* so common in Ontario in abandoned fields, burnt-over areas or open slopes. The most common Canadian fern, it's considered a weed. By contrast, just down the road to the cottage, Aileen spotted the rarer rattlesnake fern (*Botrychium virginianum*), centre frond rising above the others, poised like the rattles on an alarmed snake. Despite keeping her eyes open on naturalists' hikes, however, Aileen says she has yet to find a hay-scented fern (*Dennstaedtia punctilobula*), which other enthusiasts tell her is common.

In recent years, Aileen Coates has organized a nature scavenger hunt for the children of the Kashawigamog Lake Organization. The youngsters scout around for leaves with toothed edges, lichen, variously shaped stones, and seeds carried by birds or wind. She believes you don't destroy what you appreciate and that children who grow up knowing the forest will want to preserve it. Already her grandson Marlon, born in 1990, can identify jewelweed and, not surprisingly, a variety of ferns for his younger brother Sammy.

Meanwhile the original clump of maidenhair fern still grows luxuriantly on the rock where Audrey Coates once pointed it out to her daughter-in-law.

❧ ENCOURAGING THE INDIGENOUS ❧

The moss garden on the rocks in front of Mukwa Lodge symbolizes cottage life on this Georgian Bay island. Julia Foster is determined to impose nothing that would interfere with the natural beauty of the surroundings.

To make the moss garden, she transplanted several mosses from nearby and planted others she brought from Labrador. In a long drought the moss will bake and turn brown, but with sufficient rain the moss garden is glorious, a cool green cushion sloping on either side of steps.

On rock closer to the dock, her daughter Jessica transplanted more moss around a water-filled basin where a frog makes its home. A large carved turtle from Thailand overlooks the rock pool.

When rock was dynamited during construction of the cottage, a small crevice opened a few steps from the deck. Julia made a cutting garden by filling the crevice with plants that look as if they belong such as yarrow, marguerites, black-eyed Susan and chamomile. She has also transplanted to the front of the cottage indigenous milkweed, sumac, astilbe, white boneset, juniper, lowbush cranberry and sedum,

bringing some plants from uninhabited outer islands farther out in the bay. Blueberry bushes are native to the island.

If further ornamentation is wanted inside the cottage, a family member may trek to a swamp on the island, picking a few water lilies to grace a wide pottery bowl, or take from a large colony of electric-blue pickerel weed a handful to stand in a birchbark vase.

The Fosters built their cottage, designed by architect Gordon Ridgley, to salute Robert Foster's British Columbia heritage. The name Mukwa Lodge was inspired by a Haida legend about a mother bear with twins. After consulting authorities at the Museum of Civilization in Hull, they commissioned artist Robert Jackson of Hazleton, British Columbia, to construct four totems for their living room.

Julia is fascinated by rocks and has brought samples from the east and west coasts of Canada to the cottage. On a remote stream near Nimmo Bay on mainland British Columbia, where she was salmon fishing without much luck, she turned to picking up smooth stones from the crystal-clear water. She collected more small rocks at Adlatok River in Labrador. As

well, she gathered beautiful examples of Labradorite picked up south of Nain. This rock, mined to make jewellery, has blue veins that sparkle, especially when immersed in water.

She was thrilled when, during construction of the cottage, a worker brought her a piece of rock shaped like the pre-Columbian sculpted heads found in parts of Central America. It takes pride of place on the smooth granite outside the living-room window.

At Georgian Bay, Julia says, "I feel the rock has so much character and personality and colour on its own. Wildflowers reinforce that. If they are bright, they are usually small, and the predominant colours go so well with the rock, the soft purples, the white." When she buys plants, she says, she asks for ones that are indigenous. She adds, "I'm not adverse to moving things around, getting more colour under my eyes, and I have moved the sumac," bringing it to the forefront.

Julia Foster notes that she, like many busy career women of her generation, doesn't have the luxury of spending the whole summer at the cottage. Her garden, primarily of indigenous plants, has as its advantages not only that it requires less maintenance than a garden of exotic imports, but also that it suits the Georgian Bay landscape.

Transplanted mosses around a rock pool complement
the natural setting at a Georgian Bay cottage.

❧ SEEDS FROM THE PAST ❧

Giant sunflowers nod over the 15-foot (3 m) wooden palisade that encloses Sainte-Marie Among the Hurons. If Maurice Desroches has his way, one summer soon he will coax scarlet runner beans to grow up another foot, over the height of the palisade.

Desroches is the agricultural artisan at Sainte-Marie, the reconstruction of a mission founded by French Jesuits in 1639 in the land of the Wendat, or Huron people. For a decade the mission served as a refuge for itinerant missionaries and Christian Wendat. Today the site on the banks of the Wye River near Midland, Ontario, a short drive from cottages on southern Georgian Bay, attracts an average of 800 visitors a day, up to 2,700 at the height of the summer.

The reconstruction includes two longhouses, a hospital, a well, a church, a shoemaker and tailor shop, a Jesuit residence, a refectory, a chapel, carpenter and blacksmith shops, stables, a cookhouse, a farmer's dwelling and granary, all constructed with tools and techniques used by the Wendat and the Europeans in the 1600s.

The three main gardens at Sainte-Marie are based on what the Wendat grew and on seventeenth-century European garden plots — cookhouse garden with vegetables and sunflowers, a medicinal herb garden, and plantings of the Three Sisters, honouring an Iroquois legend of three sister spirits who guarded corn, beans and squash.

Jesuit journals, diaries of explorers such as Champlain, and archaeological digs yield evidence of what would have

A planting at Sainte-Marie Among the Hurons honours a legend about three spirit sisters who guarded corns beans and squash.

been grown. When the Jesuits and some of their Wendat followers, expecting an attack from the Iroquois, abandoned Sainte-Marie in the spring of 1648, they set it afire. Some archaeobotanical studies have been done on charred plant remains, which are almost indestructable if buried soon after burning.

Maurice Desroches, who grew up on a nearby farm, is determined that the gardens should reflect historical reality. He is especially pleased to be using seeds of ancient lineage from Central America and France. At the same time, like any gardener, he takes pride in producing the biggest and best vegetables he can. Maurice pushes the limits of the growing season. One year he chanced frost by planting the first section of the cookhouse garden May 9. Raised beds, which originated in Europe, warm the soil for earlier planting.

In a back area, Maurice tends two gargantuan compost piles. He transports kitchen waste from the restaurant, grass clippings, bedding from the paddock and barnyard, pine needles, shavings and sawdust from the building area, manure from chicken coops and the pig run, and scrap vegetation. He turns the piles every day and every spring adds compost to the gardens, already located on prime land that the Wendat had chosen.

The cookhouse garden, with its field peas, beans, squash, corn and herbs, combines the expertise of the Wendat, a settled agricultural society, and the Jesuits' knowledge of European plants. Located far from sources of European supply,

In a recreated seventeenth-century cookhouse garden, sunflowers tower over corn and climbing beans.
The gardener seeks out seeds of appropriate lineage.

the Jesuits were dependent on Wendat knowledge and largely adopted their diet, though the priests also brought livestock from Quebec by canoe. Maurice is in charge of livestock at Sainte-Marie, including razorback pigs, Houdan hens and Canadienne cattle.

For the Three Sisters, Maurice plants corn seed in a circular mound about two weeks before the bean and squash seeds. Since chipmunks dig up the seeds, he sometimes replants the corn hills two or three times. As they grow, the beans twine up the corn stalks while the squash leaves smother grass and weeds at the base.

Maurice says the Wendat cleared land by girdling trees of their bark one year and burning them the next. The resulting ash provided fertilizer. Native women and children planted and tended the crops, Maurice notes, and the Wendat likely had a dog that would chase animals away. He has used live traps to get rid of raccoons, groundhogs and squirrels. A fence now surrounds the cookhouse garden, discouraging some animal invaders.

Corn, it's believed, was developed from grasses in Mexico and moved northeast as plant breeders adapted it to cooler climates. It was grown in Southern Ontario before A.D. 1000. Among agricultural people such as the Wendat, corn leaves were woven into mats, masks and slippers, the hollowed stalk stored medicines, rough cobs made scrub brushes, and shredded husks could be used for bedding. Corn on the cob was baked, boiled, or fried in bear grease and also made into soup. Women pounded dried corn into flour for bread or stuffed it into deerskin pouches for travel.

Archaeological evidence suggests that corn made up about 65 percent of the Huron diet, beans 13 percent and squash 2 percent, providing enough complete protein for all but expectant mothers and newly weaned toddlers. Certainly the Huron were described as a strong and healthy people before they were decimated by European diseases.

Maurice has planted several kinds of beans likely grown in the 1600s, the most authentic perhaps a reddish purple-and-orange Mexican bean. Some of his bean pods have reached 16 inches (40 cm). Large broad beans are grown from seeds that originated in Europe and South America. Rather than reaching for a fungicide when a fungus attacked the beans, he removed the blackened ones by hand.

Maurice also cultivates the indigenous highbush cranberry and turnips, which were grown in Europe in the seventeenth century. In another area, he grows flax, used historically to make linen fibre, and tobacco. Smoking tobacco had become a common habit in North America by 1350.

The Wendat used sunflower seeds mainly for their oil; seeds appeared dating back to between 1300 and 1400 in garbage dumps unearthed by archaeologists in Ontario. The Wendat also consumed berries, wild onions, ground nuts, skunk cabbage and maple syrup.

The apothecary garden adjacent to the hospital at Sainte-Marie features herbs such as chicory, wormwood, lemon balm, woodruff, rue, catnip, sage, thyme, hyssop, garlic and mint. These would have been sown by the apothecary to make medicines used in European treatment at the time. As well, it's likely that Dr. Francois Gendron, who arrived at the mission from France in 1643, would have gained knowledge of indigenous remedies such as boiled cedar for dysentery.

Maurice says the Wendat always kept a three-year cache of seed in hidden spots in the forest so that in the event of drought or early frost, they would never be without seed. He harvests seeds from the best of the plants at Sainte-Marie and keeps a supply in a dry room. This selection not only helps produce gigantic sunflowers and beans but enables him to preserve the old strains of seeds entrusted to Sainte-Marie Among the Hurons.

Maurice Desroche's work on the reconstruction of the one-time mission garden has a parallel among gardeners and farmers elsewhere who are engaged in preserving the diversity of plants by collecting and planting heritage seeds.

❧ HELPING NATURE IN HALIBURTON ❧

Looking down through the treetops from their hillcrest home above Mountain Lake in Haliburton, Lynn and Ed Hancock cherish the serenity. "I think it just makes you feel you're part of the universe or creation, in touch with what really matters," says Lynn Hancock.

She sees the lot as naturally landscaped, so much of her gardening involves uncovering and highlighting the indigenous plants. She weeds around trilliums and spring beauties (*Claytonia*) but doesn't transplant them, although she planted daffodil bulbs to add to the spring scene under the trees. On a flat area near the lake, she cleared away dead brush and uncovered bearberry, huge patches of bluebead lily, Solomon's seal and Canada May apple. Between the road and the house, the undergrowth rose over their heads. Clearing for flower beds, Hancock pulled out plants by hand to make sure she didn't destroy native plants such as wild asters.

In one sunny bed, she adds begonias annually to the perennial primroses, coneflower, iris, delphiniums, coral bells, phlox, calla lilies, citron geranium, white storksbill (*Erodium variable Album*), purple rock-cress and foxgloves. Near the driveway, coneflower, violets, false Solomon's seal, hosta, fern, lupines and a pink-and-white bleeding heart make a green, pink and blue palette. In a side bed, delphiniums, iris, sweet William, tulips, cosmos, hen and chickens, nasturtiums and snapdragons from seed meet the edge of the woods.

The Hancocks discovered Mountain Lake long before it was developed when they brought their son to a hockey camp in the area. In 1970 they bought their steep lot primarily for the views that Ed Hancock wanted to paint. For years, they rented a cottage and walked along the shore to their lot for picnics. They started building their house in 1985 and moved in the following year.

Lynn Hancock, who always had flower gardens in the city, joined the Minden and District Horticultural Society and is on the executive. Ed Hancock, who paints landscapes and native plants in oil, watercolours and acrylics, was invited to open his studio for the annual Haliburton studio tour.

They began terracing the slope in front of the house with rocks that Ed moved — "hernia city," he says. Rock paths wind down to the lake past beds of Shasta daisies, black-eyed Susans, purple coneflower and flame-coloured gaillardia. Above one retaining wall, petunias and marigolds highlight a sweep of goutweed. "Risking my life," crawling around gardening on the incline, has given Lynn the nickname "the human fly."

A hillside garden blends perennials such as these with indigenous plants for a natural look.

In spring a colony of wild blue phlox (*Phlox divaricata*) lights up a patch of the hillside, and in summer the pink-flowering bull thistle and Queen Anne's lace bloom where they come up. "They were already here to grace the ground, just waiting for someone to recognize them."

Lynn doesn't use fertilizer. She credits compost for the vigour of her cultivars. Back in the '50s when her compost pile was the only one in her

Cottage gardeners frequently recommend daisylike plants
such as these black-eyed Susans and purple coneflower, grown in Haliburton.

city neighbourhood, horrified neighbours warned her it would attract rats.

In Haliburton a friend who boards horses saves manure for her; she adds a layer of it to composted green waste from the kitchen and weeds picked before they go to seed. All this is layered with leaves. "I save every leaf that falls," she says. "Some of the people around here actually haul leaves to the Ingoldsby dump." Before adding bushels of compost to the flower beds spring and fall, she sifts the compost; material that's not ready goes back on the pile.

On the deck overlooking the lake, Lynn fills containers with petunias and geraniums that she keeps going from year to year. Frost arrives several weeks later at Mountain Lake than in nearby Minden, thanks to the moderating influence of the lake and the higher elevation. Nasturtiums and bachelor buttons last well into the fall.

Bringing the geraniums indoors each fall, she cuts them low and lets them dry in a bushel basket. In February she soaks them for an hour or so in a laundry tub to "soften" them before potting indoors, in preparation for the summer.

The Hancocks, married more than fifty years, sit on the deck watching the birds they feed in all seasons — jays, hummingbirds, warblers. "I feel it's just a privilege to live here," Lynn Hancock says.

❧ Finding What Works ❧

Ground covers such as periwinkle and creeping phlox are giving way to foamflower, partridge berry, wintergreen, Canada Mayflower and ferns at the Bergsma cottage on Lake Rosseau. The garden is in transition, from a reliance on cultivated plants to native.

Marie Bergsma's father bought the property, which extends from a waterfall edging Clark's Pond to shoreline on Lake Rosseau, in the 1940s. Marie and Fred Bergsma built their cottage in 1975. They left the vast majority of the property in its original state, but introduced some plants near the cottage.

Their children, Brian, Michael, John and Bonnie, spent their summers swimming, catching frogs and crayfish, and developing a love of the outdoors. While they are all naturalists, Bonnie went on to become a botanist and ecologist, the perfect person for her parents to consult about plants.

Initially, Marie Bergsma put in periwinkle and creeping phlox, but she says if she were starting a garden at the cottage now she would begin with indigenous alternatives because they are "easy care," adapted to their surroundings, and look pretty. Now that her foamflower has spread, for example, she likes it better than periwinkle.

The waxy, green-centred flowers of native pipsissewa bloom from June to August. This specimen grows on a wooded slope at a Lake Rosseau cottage.

"A lot of [cultivated] ground covers are quite invasive," her daughter notes, citing lily of the valley, periwinkle and goutweed. As a ground cover, sweet woodruff is fine if confined to the garden, but if it's bordering on the woods, she would take it out. Often there's a native counterpart to the cultivar, and in the case of sweet woodruff, it's fragrant bedstraw (*Galium triflorum*). For lily of the valley, a substitute is Canada Mayflower (*Maianthemum canadense*), also known as wild lily of the valley.

Near the cottage in the garden where she started, Marie grows a mixture of cultivated and native plants, including spiderwort, coral bells, saxifrage (*Bergenia cordifolia*), astilbe, meadow rue, wild iris (*Iris versicolor*), violets, ferns, Canada Mayflower, and bunchberry (*Cornus canadensis*).

Around the cottage, Bonnie says, perennials and annuals can be used "to get the colour up," but for transition areas next to the forest, she advocates native plants. There's no shortage of colour around the Bergsmas' cottage. Annuals in containers brighten the deck and doorways. Near the cottage primroses, yellow coreopsis, purple-flowering hosta, purple coneflower and pastel astilbe add spring and summer colour. Elsewhere in the garden, Marie grows a cultivar of phlox and native plants, some of which were there to begin with, including marginal woodfern, enchanter's nightshade (*Circaea lutetiana*), foamflower, phlox and native doll's-eye (*Actaea pachypoda*). The edge of the driveway is defined with a line of daylilies and irises on one side, astilbe on the other. The native pagoda dogwood (*Cornus alternifolia*), spotted jewelweed (*Impatiens capensis*), ostrich fern and native sedges mark a transition to the forest.

For trees, Bonnie Bergsma advises sticking to natives. "There are so many beautiful ones." She says it's best to resist the urge to rake and sweep everything out of the forest. "You have to leave some small saplings to replace large trees and even leave dead trees if you want woodpeckers."

Yet you can take down certain branches to create "windows" for a view, Marie adds. Her husband, Fred, says that, depending on the way the wind blows, taking down whole trees can create wind corridors, making other trees more vulnerable to storms and scalding the understorey. Judicious pruning helps prevent these problems.

On the east side of the cottage, astilbe, Oregon grape and hosta grow in a cultivated area. The red-berried elderberry (*Sambucus racemosa pubens*), common polypody fern, wild sarsaparilla (*Aralia nudicaulis*), bush honeysuckle (*Diervilla lonerica*), juniper and blueberry grow naturally. By the stairs to the lake, bluebead lily, columbine (*Aquilegia canadensis*) and foamflower grow, with pink-flowered pipsissiwa (*Chimaphila umbellata*) farther down the slope.

To those who find wildflowers as a whole rather inconspicuous, Bonnie says it's amazing how these plants can be encouraged by improving the soil. But unsterilized topsoil is likely to contain a whole seedbed of species not native to the area. She advises, if you must import soil, letting the weeds germinate in the pile of topsoil before spreading and killing them with glysophate, a herbicide sold as Roundup.

She has talked to landscapers who complain that people are buying cottage properties without considering the landscape, exposure and animals, and then expecting to garden. "If you buy a hemlock forest and want gardens, it's going to be really hard to do, because the soils are not good for that." And chopping down hemlock and cedar along the shore removes important cover for animals such as mink.

One landscaper with whom she recently worked had a client who wanted to install a stairway while preserving the natural topsoil and plants around it. Bonnie helped to save the vegetation that would otherwise have been destroyed by construction. They made a temporary nursery in a shady area under hemlocks. When the stairs were completed, the native plants and soil were replaced. The effect was as if the stairs had always been there.

The Bergsmas have transplanted onto their property hepatica, false Solomon's seal, bloodroot (*Sanguinaria canadensis*), Jack-in-the-pulpit, and shinleaf (*Pyrola elliptica*), which has green-veined flowers followed by red berries.

When transplanting, take only from an environment on your property where lots of the plants are growing, Bonnie says. And take a whole soil ball, since the plants might depend on the microorganisms in the soil. If there's only one plant, it's best not to move it; it may be rare.

Bergsma was one of the authors of the Natural Heritage Evaluation of Muskoka, which includes a species list of all plants, native and introduced, and those rare in the district, provincially or nationally. The study lists vascular plants, mushrooms, birds, mammals, herpetofauna (such as snakes, frogs, salamanders and turtles), butterflies and dragonflies in the district.

An afternoon canoe trip that's become an annual family event gives the Bergsmas an opportunity to observe the neighbouring natural flora and fauna. Starting at Three Mile Lake, they paddle down the Dee River into tranquil Clark's Pond. At the far end of the pond there's a portage right beside the waterfall that tumbles down into Lake Rosseau, at a spot adjacent to their property. The scenery on the outing represents the kind of Muskoka the family wants to preserve.

Animals aren't intimidated by this peaceful setting.

Chapter 5
Animals

The orange flash of a Northern Oriole, the thwack of a beaver's tail on the lake, the chipmunk's silky striped pelt, even the scent of a skunk — at a distance — all these evoke life at the cottage. Yet it's downright discouraging to find young pines repeatedly nibbled into bonsai by deer, a vegetable crop harvested overnight by chipmunks, hare or raccoons, or flowers stripped to the stalk by a groundhog. Cottage owners' reactions to wild creatures can veer from delight to outrage.

Alan Watson, director of the Arboretum at the University of Guelph, draws a grid to illustrate how interactions viewed negatively from the human perspective increase with gardening effort. The vertical line on the left of the grid represents negative animal interactions. The horizontal line at the bottom stands for gardening effort — on the left, leaving the wild as is, and moving to the right, increased use of cultivars, vegetable plantings, lawns and exotic plants. As gardening effort increases, animal interactions seen as negative rise. The further from the wild the gardener goes, the greater the work required to repel and outwit the animals.

Some people still resort to shotguns, poisons and traps, but most of the gardeners in this book preferred not to kill another living creature. Live-trapping and relocating the animal to another area may seem a considerate control, but naturalists say this isn't the best solution. The removed animal may leave a nest and helpless young behind and be unable to compete for food with the established animal population in its new home.

Here are some techniques, admittedly labour-intensive, that are based on animal behaviour:

DEER

Deer can devastate a garden overnight, consuming fruit, vegetables, foliage and flowers. Since they tend to follow the same trails year after year, it's possible to observe their tracks in the snow then site the garden away from their path. Single deer fences have to be at least 12 feet (3.6 m) high. Two 4-foot-high (1.2 m) fences of 2-by-4-inch (5 by 10 cm) mesh attached to metal stakes and placed 5 feet (1.5 m) apart will also be effective. If building a wooden fence, leave spaces of less than 2 inches (5 cm) between boards, since deer like to see what's on the other side before they leap.

Some people claim success with folk remedies such as hair (the hair is supposed to be replaced every three days) or deodorant soap placed at deer nose-height, about 30 inches (76 cm) above the ground, every 3 feet (91 cm) around the garden. These are hardly ornamental solutions.

BEAVER

Beaver will eat aspen, poplar and birch before maple or pine, so keep that in mind if you are planting trees. Physical barriers may deter beaver. Metal chain-link fencing or square poultry mesh, stiffer than round mesh, should be attached to a hoop and a metal stake and moved up as the tree grows.

RACCOONS

If you have fish in a water garden, put in sections of plastic pipe 1 1/2 inches (4 cm) in diameter and 12 to 15 inches (30 40 cm) long, so fish can seek shelter when a raccoon fancies them for supper. Depending on the size of the pond, you could cover it with wire mesh held in place by a bungee cord. No fence, electrified or not, will keep out raccoons.

GROUNDHOGS

When fencing a vegetable garden, bend the mesh in a J-shape underground, with the J bending back away from the garden. A groundhog, if it hits a curve, will not turn around and burrow underneath.

SNOWSHOE HARE

Hare will nibble bark from young trees and shrubs, herbaceous plants, carrots, grasses, lettuce, peas, raspberry canes and tulip shoots. A regular chicken-wire fence, though hardly attractive, will keep hares out, and individual cylinders of galvanized hardware cloth higher than 1 1/2 feet (45 cm) can protect individual plants. Clear away brush piles near the garden. They are favourite hiding spots for hares in the daytime. A good planting of clover offers an alternative food source. With luck, the hare will stuff itself so full of clover it won't go for the carrots.

MICE AND VOLES

Mice and voles may spend the winter in mulch placed around perennials, chewing on the roots. If possible, return to the cottage after the ground has frozen hard to apply mulch. Around valued trees, keep the land clear of shrubs and tall grass that provide shelter, since mice and voles hesitate to cross open land. Of course, snakes eat mice and voles, and a rock pile encourages snakes. You could also try baiting a large number of snap traps for several nights before setting them off all at once.

SQUIRRELS

Pepper and commercial repellents need to be reapplied to plants after a rainfall. When planting, keep in mind that squirrels will not consume the bulbs of daffodils.

Canada geese may be a nuisance in city parks but are welcome in this Stony Lake garden.

INSECTS

Encourage insect predators such as bats, toads and songbirds to take up residence in the garden by providing houses for them. Deciduous and coniferous shrubs offer birds nesting sites, cover and food.

SLUGS AND SNAILS

Sharp-edged eggshells and diatomaceous earth create an uncomfortable barrier for slugs and snails. Or you could try a 2-inch (5 cm) band of flexible copper sheeting wrapped around the timbers on a raised bed or on the outside of planters to give slugs and snails an electric shock. Separating plants such as hosta so that air can circulate and dry up the damp will discourage snails and slugs, and many gardeners give them a happy death in a saucer of beer.

ATTRACTING BUTTERFLIES

Butterflies are more likely to visit a garden that presents protection from wind with a wall, fence or shrub hedge. A few flat stones in a sunny location provide a relaxation spot, and butterflies appreciate a sheltered water source.

Columbines, achillea species, sneezeweed, centaurea species and phlox offer the vibrant colour so entrancing to butterflies. They feed on nectar of sweet peas, dame's rocket, honeysuckle, hollyhock, verbena, Joe-Pye-weed and pinks. Aside from leaving a patch of milkweed for monarch larvae, many of us would not think of food for the caterpillar stage. Gardeners can provide borage, parsley, dill, carrot, fennel and nasturtium for butterfly larvae. A true enthusiast would plant stinging nettles.

In this chapter and elsewhere in the book, you will meet gardeners who have tried a variety of techniques to encourage the coexistence of animals and garden plants.

❧ DON'T EXPECT A CITY GARDEN ❧

Most of us would have stepped on it without a thought, a tiny plant almost hugging the ground. Biologist R. D. (Ron) Lawrence bent down and pointed out a miniscule patch of sundew, one of the few carnivorous plants in Canada, growing naturally at his property in Haliburton.

Ron Lawrence believes that native trees, Solomon's seal, false Solomon's seal, milkweed, and trout lilies, also called dogtooth violets, bunchberry, honeysuckles, twin flowers, touch-me-nots and wild mushrooms make a natural landscape that's hard to beat.

After forty years of observing the natural life of animals, Ron speaks with assurance about some of the animals that cottage gardeners may consider pests. If you have property in an area with many green fields and little forest, there's not a lot you can do about animals helping themselves to your vegetable garden, he says. Deprived of their own food base, they are actually being trained to eat farm produce. Corn farmers hate raccoons, but humans have created the problem by clearing everything away, leaving little natural habitat for raccoons. Likewise, snowshoe hare, if they find sufficient food in the bush, are less likely to gobble the gardener's lettuce and carrots.

His wife, Sharon, advocates leaving clover, plantain and dandelion leaves in place for hares to consume. Raccoons may best be lured from plants with table scraps or a combination of dog food and peanuts and stale bread, always put in the same place every day, Ron says.

The indigenous cardinal flower provides natural food for hummingbirds and butterflies.

If you insist on trying to put a city lawn into the country, however, raccoons and skunks will likely dig up the dirt to find June bug larvae, which they consume like candy. Raccoons and skunks are beneficial to lawns, because they eat the larvae that feed on grass roots. If the holes left by the skunks and raccoons are covered again by the gardener, the grass will soon grow over the disturbed patch of earth.

When you find deer nibbling on ornamental plants, it probably indicates an overpopulation of deer or a dearth of their natural foods, Ron says. Clear-cutting drives them out onto roads and onto settled properties. A high fence around the garden may be the only solution.

As for red squirrels, trapping and moving them some distance from the garden could be detrimental, he says, if the squirrels have to leave nests behind, or if the new location doesn't have the right habitat. A mesh tent over plants you especially want to preserve will protect them from many animals, adds Sharon, who lost an expensive clump of lilies to animals several years ago.

Ron snorts with laughter at the widely held notion that pissing human urine around the boundaries of a garden will deter bears. The myth is one of many about animal behaviour; it's more likely that the ammonia in urine would attract the bears as to a cadaver.

Author of 29 books on animals and plants published in 13 languages in 17 countries, Ron Lawrence holds strong opinions about gardening in the wild. Don't come up north from Toronto and

The miniscule sundew is one of Canada's few carnivorous plants.

expect to recreate a beautiful well-tended garden like you have at home, he warns. "It's impossible when you're living in a natural system to change that system into a civilized garden." If someone wants to grow native plants in the region where they already grow, Ron sees nothing wrong, though he cautions that some native plants transplant well and others not at all.

Because Ron spends a good part of his time writing and Sharon is usually busy with other tasks, they do not have much time for gardening. Most years, depending on the weather, they put in a vegetable garden behind the house. They also enjoy easy-care perennials such as phlox, heliopsis, purple coneflower, liatris, black-eyed Susan, daylilies and rhubarb in a sheltered spot against an outbuilding.

Ron Lawrence contends that most of the problems with animals that occur in the garden are caused by the gardeners themselves, when they provide new plants for birds, mammals and insects in search of food. In nature, he cautions, everything is connected to everything else.

Raccoons congregate on the grass for their nightly feeding.

❧ ANIMALS WELCOME HERE ❧

To arrive at the Guillet garden on Stony Lake, a boat navigates through a narrow entrance to a marsh, at a spot where beaver frequently try dam-building. A family of Canada geese paddles serenely in the marsh, which is spiked with cattails and pickerel weed. Among shimmering water lilies a still blue heron waits patiently for prey.

It's a fitting introduction to the garden, which is a haven for animals. Jeannie Guillet says she and her husband, Rob, allow everything that wants to live around the area into the garden, believing the animals have a right to the land. In fact, they encourage the animals, feeding chipmunks and red squirrels and in the winter, deer. After someone brought them two raccoons to raise, another sat up a tree looking enviously at the dog food, so they began feeding it too. By the mid-90s, thirty raccoons were appearing nightly on the grass for food, creating a "fur lawn that moves."

Jeannie says one neighbour has complained that "her" raccoons are visiting, but she believes they stay close to the spot where they are fed. She was reassured by another friend who advised, "If you want to have an animal garden as well as a plant garden, go right ahead."

To discourage rodents from eating spring bulbs, Jeannie plants them late in the fall and covers them with a pile of straw. She has observed that groundhogs don't like succulents, cleome, lupines or delphiniums, although deer will nibble delphiniums as well as Japanese maples. A porcupine wandering through devastated a fir tree. If Jeannie tries a vegetable garden in future, however, she plans to discourage animals with a close-gapped picket fence sunk down into cement and possibly a low-voltage electric fence at the perimeter.

The Guillets bought the house in 1985, after the previous owner had dredged part of the marshy arm of the lake for access to the property. The gardens are well protected from the wind by trees, but despite proximity to the marsh, mosquitoes are not a problem. The black soil heaped on the shoreline provided an accessible rich base for the gardens.

Having gardened in England and Chile, Jeannie Guillet knew what she wanted — an English-style garden that embraces both cultivated perennials and plants of the wild, such as goldenrod and milkweed. She tried hard not to have a sharp division between the garden and the wild.

To shape two large beds on the lawn, she laid out garden hose in arcing curves and judged the effect from a large upstairs window. The outline established, she began filling in with wheelbarrows of earth that had once been in the marsh.

Guillet plants in groupings, so the eye is carried from one clump to another. She mixes annuals such as cosmos and coleus with perennials — white, red and pink astilbe, peonies, yellow yarrow, hosta, veronica, sedum, lily of the valley, an upright lysimachia and goldenrod. A purple-leafed sandcherry provides three-season interest. In a second bed, she put in iris, pink sedum, astilbe, lupines, peonies, phlox, hostas, loosestrife and evening primrose with a silver dogwood for accent. Violets fringe the front edges.

Near the kitchen, a herb garden spills over with, among many plants, garlic chives, nasturtiums, Italian parsley and coneflower. Down by the dock, the garden is expanding. Cleome self-seeded, eight plants one year eventually increasing to sixty-six. The astilbe stands nearly as tall as Jeannie does. Robust rhubarb flourishes.

Jeannie has a busy life outside the garden and says she's not a dedicated gardener, but she is enjoying the trial and error process. She's lucky if she can give the garden an hour or two a day, although in the spring it requires more time.

🌿 DISCOURAGING DEER 🌿

Whether it's golf, boating, or collecting antique sports equipment, Bill Bartels tackles his hobbies energetically — and gardening is no exception.

Bill insists he's not knowledgeable about gardening, but he enjoys working at it. He credits his father-in-law, Maurice Beaver, with starting him off at a city home. "He got me going on it, showed me how to put a plant in." Bartels then created a garden at the first cottage he and his wife, Eileen, bought in Muskoka in the '80s.

After buying Harraby Point on Lake Rosseau in 1991, he had stone walkways put through the property to the boathouse, using no concrete. The stone, already home to lichen and some low-growing phlox, looks as if it has been there for decades. Some garden beds were in place, and he consulted Doreen Butson of Port Carling on the layout of other beds. She also recommended Victorian-style urns for the front deck. He fills them with annuals such as pink geraniums, draceana, ivy and purple scaevola.

Ferns, roses and astilbe grow beside the porch steps on one side. On the other side, Froebel's spirea, a begonia bed in red, orange and yellow, palm trees, and lilies of pink, yellow, white and salmon are spread underneath pine and oak trees. Farther along the rock pathway, flower beds give way to pines, oak, cedar and an understorey of big-leafed aster.

Bill estimates that he puts in two weeks of heavy work in the spring. One summer, for example, he planted 108 tuberous begonias in a bed by the porch. He likes to get annuals in as early as he can, otherwise the selection at his favourite local nursery diminishes and he has to "go south" for plants.

At the start of the season, he fertilizes plants once a week for a month, then reduces the frequency. Until early August, he sprays on a garlic-based plant enhancer once every three weeks. The theory is it strengthens the plant and fertilizes

A deer fence, not seen in the picture, protects a prized begonia bed and other plantings at Lake Rosseau.

through the leaves. To assess moisture, "I kind of stick my finger in the soil," and he waters when it's needed. After planting, "weeding is the big thing."

When deer came onto the property regularly to chew plants, Bill tried folk remedies such as sticks with soap on them, and hair brushed from his son's dog and spread all over. Neither technique deterred the deer, so he recently erected an electric fence, actually two separate fences meeting at the front gate and running down both sides of the point to the lake. The fence, 5 feet (1.5 m) high, extends "a couple of thousand feet" and had to be rebuilt after the heavy snows of 1995–96. "In the summer, we close the gate every night, that's the deer control. Touch wood, we haven't seen one this year. Now we got these rabbits this year, a family of five, they just strip plants."

Bill has been observing other animals in relation to plants. He finds that raccoons and porcupines don't hurt garden plants but porcupines will damage trees, pipes and wires. He has tried growing water lilies, ten big buckets of them between a dock and the shore. But only one grew one year and two the next. "Something's eating them."

Much of the point remains in its natural state, with velvety green moss, juniper and wild blueberry bushes. "Some people come up [to a cottage] and think they should tear everything out — they ruin it," he observes. On the rocky point, several flower beds are spread out in vivid colours, one of white nicotiana and red fibrous begonias, another with yellow marigolds and blue ageratum, and a third glowing with blue

A deer fence, not seen in the picture, protects a prized begonia bed and other plantings at Lake Rosseau.

delphiniums, yellow marigolds, hosta, vetch and daisies. In another planting, backed by tall yellow-flowering heliopsis, he combines begonias, geraniums and creeping Jennie (*Lysimachia nummularia*).

Window boxes at the boat-house hold blue browallia, pink geraniums, purple scaevola and white alyssum.

At a swimming area along the shore on the other side of the property, two turreted towers in grey and white with pink trim contain showers and a sauna; between them on the deck is an open-air hot tub backed by a pleasing display of pink and white impatiens and grey licorice plant. Nearby, a bridge joins the mainland to a small island with a log cabin they named Brudvik Cabin in honour of a friend, a Scandinavian sea captain; Bill says it was once an Indian trading post.

Eileen Bartels likes perennials, and one of her favourite books is *The Secret Garden*, the 1910 novel by Frances Hodgson Burnett. So one of the best-disguised septic beds in Muskoka is known as "Eileen's Secret Garden." It's between the cottage and the gate, and surrounded by a white picket fence, built by the Bartels' son, Scott, to his father's specifications. The garden blooms in pastel hues from June to September with tulips, peonies, iris, sweet William, daisies, delphiniums, phlox, purple coneflower, lamb's ears and Autumn Joy sedum.

The Bartels are hoping that the deer fence will protect the secret garden and the other gardens developed in a scant half-decade at Harraby Point.

Reflections of astilbe, hosta and tuberous begonias glimmer in Lake Joseph.
The vegetable garden is enclosed by a fence to deter animals.

🌿 BARRIERS AS PROTECTION 🌿

Green whorls of hosta, plumes of astilbe, trumpets of lilies and clusters of yellow, pink and red tuberous begonias glisten along the shoreline. Window boxes brim with bright annuals at the dock and boathouse. Hydrangea, ferns, hosta, white astilbe, bergenia, lamb's ears, sedum and ajuga carpet the ground beside stone walkways. Perennial and vegetable gardens surround the house.

This is, Jeff Reid hastens to say, not a typical cottage garden. It's a full-time occupation for him and his wife, Linda.

The Reids, who had been in the garden centre business in the city, relocated to Lake Joseph in 1989 and began landscaping at once. Although you may see timbers and brickwork on cottage lots, rocks are the natural way to landscape in Muskoka, says Jeff, who spent boyhood summers at a family cottage on Lake Joe. Section by section, beginning around their new house and moving out, the Reids had stone walkways installed, then began adding soil. Perennials were chosen to survive the severe winters and often wet summers.

Not long afterward, they opened Hemlock Hill Gardens, a greenhouse business where many of their cottage neighbours come to buy annuals and perennials. The Reids close for the season before the end of July and return to full-time work on their own gardens. Jeff says it's a continual job moving perennials around to the right locations, wherever it's not too wet, too dry, too sunny or too shaded. If you keep weeds under control, he says, they are a problem only for the first couple of years.

Jeff planted a vegetable garden in layers of soil on a septic bed in full sun, where he grows "pretty well any-thing except melons because of the slightly cooler, wetter season." In the summer, garlic, corn, beets, Boston lettuce, onions, broccoli, spinach, green peppers, cucumbers, zucchini, bush beans, beans and tomatoes arrive at the table. "We grow our own winter supply of potatoes, squash, onions and carrots," adds Linda.

Finding animals competing for the plants, they installed an electric fence to discourage deer. "It's not as if you're shooting them; it's really quite harmless." To discourage animals from harvesting the crops, the vegetable garden is enclosed in a chain-link fence. Outside the chain link, the Reids plant squash and potatoes and grow rhubarb, raspberries and strawberries. Groundhogs have proven persistent, so the Reids trapped and relocated some of them, but they haven't yet found a way of discouraging moles. And they are on the lookout for some animal, one that makes a hole in the ground about an inch (2.5 cm) in diameter. Whatever it is, it has been eating the blooms off marigolds.

In several beds they grow a wide variety of perennials, including a polygonum with thick, waxy green foliage and a pink, spike-shaped flower that blooms in June. As they are on a lakefront lot and sheltered from wind, they find they can plant as early as May 10. Flowers usually last into October, with the first frost arriving weeks later than it does away from the lake. With so much moisture, Linda says, the mini-climate is almost tropical. "Hostas, daylilies and astilbes are the backbone of our gardens," Jeff says.

Sedum stands out beside stone walkways.
These gardeners use astilbe, bergenia, ferns, hosta,
ajuga and hydrangea as ground covers.

But you need annuals, insists Linda, and container gardening is certainly easier at the cottage, especially if you lack good flower beds. Annuals are so versatile, she enthuses, because you can change colours every year, although, she adds tactfully, you do see cottages with the same colours every year, and red with green and dark brown buildings is "fabulous."

For window boxes, the Reids are always after new ideas, and by the mid-'90s were keen on bidens, a yellow spreading plant, the blue-flowering vine scaveola, cascading Surfinia petunias that come in red, fuchsia, blue and pink, and two kinds of *Helichrysum*, one a strawflower plant with feathery foliage and bright yellow blooms, the other licorice plant, with trailing grey foliage.

Linda likes a cheerful mix in window boxes. At the boathouse, one window box holds variegated ivies, ivy geraniums, lobelia, blue salvia Victoria, dusty miller, dwarf nicotiana and dwarf marigolds. She recommends diacia, brachycomb with purple daisylike flowers, and bacopa, a little white feathery trailing plant.

In containers, she says, it's important to use a lightweight soilless mix, which doesn't get water-logged like peatmoss and can be left from year to year. She recommends starting with a liquid feed at least once a week at the beginning of the season. Regular watering is also important, sometimes twice a day in hanging baskets.

On their front door the Reids hang a ceramic sign that says Out in the Garden. For at least six months of the year, that's usually where they are. Judging by the lushness of their gardens, the barriers the Reids have erected to keep animals from harvesting the plants work well at this site.

🌿 WILDLIFE IN THE GARDEN 🌿

This is, Babs Carr declares, the third garden she has hacked out of the bush. The first she terraced on a slope about 380 feet (114 m) long and 40 feet (12 m) wide on Trout Lake Road near North Bay. The second she created in rough bush at Lake Nosbinsing, south of Callander, Ontario. In 1989, when the Carrs bought their present woodland lot on Chub Lake Road south of Huntsville, she planned to enjoy the wildlife and limit gardening to containers on the deck.

Spruce and other conifers offered shelter for birds in winter and protection against hawks. She planted honeysuckle bushes and vines to entice birds and butterflies. Wooden and ceramic bird-feeders suspended from trees and bushes attracted evening grosbeaks, pine grosbeaks and even redbreasted grosbeaks, which, she believes, are appearing farther north as their habitat to the south is destroyed. "A lot of grouse come to feed and mourning doves will pick up the wild birdseed that has fallen on the ground."

Perhaps inevitably for someone who has been gardening and studying horticulture for years, Babs couldn't resist planting beyond the decks. "We already had native plants, spring beauties (*Claytonia caroliniana*) and quite a few trilliums, and in spring the whole side is blue with violets." She believes a woodland garden is more in keeping with where they live than a lawn would be. Babs says her neighbours spend a

A birdbath, feeders and conifers planted for shelter encourage birds at a woodland garden where the owners also see deer, raccoons and skunks.

lot of their time cutting grass, while remarking on how busy she is in the garden. "But it's not really work, gardening." The Carrs never planted grass seed, although for three years they tried sod on a tile bed in front of the house. It was too shady for the grass and Babs wasn't sorry.

She grows roses in the dappled sunlight at the front of the house where trees provide a windbreak. Among her roses, Fairy Princess, a resilient Canadian, and the miniature Apricot Doll are favourites. She doesn't use pesticides anywhere, but dusts the roses for blackspot.

On the sunny side of the house, Babs planted spirea, climbing clematis, drifts of baby's breath, daylilies, lavender, Shasta daisies, rugosa roses, dahlias, pink balloonflower (*Platycodon grandiflorum*), white yarrow, salmon-colored oriental poppies and also red bergamot, which has expanded to ninety blooms. Across the path leading to the back, she grows ground covers, silvery thyme, sedums, lavender, creeping and upright phlox, prostrate junipers, accented in season with dwarf iris and yarrow. On a rocky outcrop beyond the back patio, she has continued with a bed of purple coneflower, yellow marguerites, Froebel's spirea, bergamot, Shastas, phlox, sedum, prostrate juniper. On an arbour she is training climbing hydrangea and wisteria.

At the deck, she hangs containers of geraniums, petunias and lobelia, and a planter near the door combines marigolds, petunias, nicotiana and white celosia. In a sunny bed by the back deck a cheerful mix of foxglove, daylilies, astilbe, Shastas,

Containers on the deck brim with marigolds, petunias, nicotiana and white celosia, under hanging baskets of geraniums, petunias and lobelia.

columbine, lavender, pinks, balloon-flower, and a dwarf blue fall aster are supplemented with annual marigolds and coleus. A clematis twines up a rugosa rose. "A lot of hummingbirds use feeders early in the spring, then move to columbine and foxgloves." With the biennial foxgloves, "I wait and watch. When they're two thirds over, I tip them over and the seeds will ripen and fall down exactly where I want them." On the shady side of the house, she grows hosta, sweet woodruff (*Asperula odoratum*), impatiens and lily of the valley.

Babs's biggest challenge is trying to keep things watered. She finds that most perennials need to be watered as often as every other day the first year to get the roots down. Among the perennials, gayfeather or liatris, which she has in white as well as purple, purple coneflower, balloon-flower and hardy asters all need to be watered well the first year, she says.

As for animals in the garden, Babs Carr reports, "A deer comes and nibbles forsythia, but deer are part of the environment. It's just a premature pruning. The forsythia is twice as big this year." She likes to see raccoons and skunks about and says her husband, Roy, with whom she celebrated a fiftieth wedding anniversary in 1995, has never killed animals. When squirrels became "an infestation," the Carrs trapped them and took them to Arrowhead Park in August, in the hope that the squirrels would still have time to gather food for the winter.

The Carrs' woodland garden, featured on the Huntsville Horticultural Society's annual garden tour, remains an all-season home for birds and animals.

Rocks to the left came out of this new garden, planted with lavender, heath and beardtongue.

🌿 THEY WERE HERE FIRST 🌿

The serenity that is fast disappearing from so many cottage locations still envelops a 16-acre (2.4 h) property on Bruce Lake in Muskoka. Nothing disturbs the quiet in the woods, at the lakeshore, or in the pastel-hued gardens where animals come and go at will.

"It's just a different atmosphere gardening here, it's so tranquil," says Peggy Harvey, who has made gardening a full-time vocation. "It's wonderful even if you're not successful all the time." She took on the challenges of animals, soil and climate, first at their A-frame cottage and later on the same acreage at their retirement home, where she began gardening even before the frame was up.

Except for a planting of Siberian iris and daylilies toward the lake, the Harveys left the shoreline alone. "We didn't want to lose the feel of Muskoka." Indigenous polypoda fern, cinnamon fern, blue flag, waterlilies and water hyacinths preserve a haven for ducks, bass and heron on fishing expeditions.

Peggy had a small city garden where "you would put something in and it would come up." When she and husband Russ first came to the cottage more than twenty years ago, she planted hyacinths, tulips and scilla in the fall. What with moles munching on the bulbs and the "horrible soil," acidic and full of tree roots, none of the bulbs grew.

As both a nature lover and a gardener, she has mixed feelings about the animals in the gardens. Chipmunks pull poppies down and eat them, and munch on tuberous begonias and geraniums. "It's so frustrating. They have a hole right beside the rosebush." Deer make their rounds every few weeks, nibbling a little here, a little there. "Russ keeps saying they were here first. I never thought I would malign deer, but I get so upset. The deer usually take a bit of each thing they fancy. They like veronica, for example. Sometimes whole herds lie down — they are wonderful to see."

Once in a while, a bear comes to the window, investigates the compost, and sips a drink from the birdbath. "He makes himself at home." A groundhog lived at the end of the garden where she used to plant vegetables for salads. "He enjoyed that."

Peggy gave up the vegetable garden near the woods, but not because of the groundhog. Tree roots robbed the soil of nutrients. "It was a choice there of trees or garden."

From the sunroom in her home at Bruce Lake, you can see her latest garden, where she planted lavender, heath, beardtongue and *Verbascum doronicum*. "This is what gardening is in Muskoka," says Peggy, waving a hand at a 15-foot-long (4.5 m) pile of rocks Russell pulled out of the soil before planting. Rocks are both a challenge and a blessing in Muskoka gardens. "We have a beautiful rock outcrop. People in England would give their eyeteeth for a setting like this."

She recommends that cottagers starting to garden begin with the soil, loosening it to at least a foot, clearing out rocks and roots and enriching it with aged sheep manure, shredded leaves and bonemeal. She also adds material from the compost heap. Because the soil already tends to the acidic, she's against using peat moss, but would add sphagnum moss if necessary.

Planting is best done in the early morning or late afternoon, she finds. She suggests that cottagers in this area choose plants hardy to Zone 4, though full-time residents who are on the scene late in the fall to cover plants for winter protection could choose Zone 5 selections. She plants and divides in the spring to give the plants a better chance. "I have always used perennials, although I put petunias in boathouse planters because they're so hardy." Peggy has a great library of gardening books and learns through reading and experience. "You have to get to know the area. It's trial and error. Some things surprise you."

From her kitchen window, she looks out on an oval garden about 20 by 10 feet (7 by 3 m) with a clump of three paper birch. Under it are bleeding heart, sweet woodruff, grape hyacinth, yellow and cream primula, a variegated grass in three clumps, false and true Solomon's seal, and Jacob's ladder.

Nearby in the shade of a pine and an oak, she has encouraged a huge clump of native bluebead lily. She planted sweet woodruff, lungwort, and Oregon grape for its yellow flowers that will match those of the bluebead lily. Hosta and ferns line steps to a latticed garden house where tools, bushel baskets and other containers are stored.

On that side of the house, a large perennial garden laid out in the shape of a four-leaf clover is divided by a lawn of grass and fragrant pennyroyal (*Mentha pulegium*). A birdbath marks the centre, and a black wrought-iron bench draws the eye to the far end.

"My garden has to be viewed from a distance," Peggy says. It's personal, not much rhyme or reason to it. You do experiment to see what nature will allow. The winters can be so different, especially last year (1995–96). I lost things I never lost before."

The four-leaf-clover-shaped garden contains coral bells, spiderwort with Jacob's ladder — "both make super cut flowers" — a scented lily that blooms in August, columbine, violets, sedum, meadow rue, the wild corydalis (*Corydalis flavula*), delphiniums, gloriosa daisy, Shasta daisy, thyme, feverfew and creeping savory (*Savory repandra*). Iris, veronica, Jerusualem artichokes, phlox, coneflower and a globe thistle

Single-flower hollyhocks grow with roses, prostrate juniper,
speedwell, arabis, bearberry and catmint
in a peaceful garden at Bruce Lake.

(*Echinops* Taplow Blue) that grows to 4 feet (1.2 m) add to the colour.

Peggy obtained seeds for single hollyhock by knocking on the door of a woman who was growing them in Bracebridge. Peonies, poppies, lamb's ears, weigela and vinca grow with a Queen Elizabeth rose which she has transplanted three times. "I won't spray."

"It's wonderful to see the hummingbirds enjoying the plants. They will go to anything with a tubular flower." She doesn't put up feeders, because she says the mixture in them isn't good for hummingbirds.

Peggy integrates indigenous plants into her gardens, encouraging wild roses that grow by the boathouse and welcoming wildflowers that seed in the garden. Solomon's seal and false Solomon's seal are "the sort of thing that's exciting." The enriched garden soil can produce amazing results; trout lilies, when cultivated, grow three times their normal size. She also finds that, for garden beds, "the ferns up here are a real standby."

On either side of the laneway approaching the Harvey place, wild apple trees, highbush cranberry, iris, buttercups, Joe-Pye-weed, birch trees, orange and yellow hawkweed and milkweed illustrate the diversity of natural growth. Near the house, Peggy planted juniper, oregano, *Lysimachia punctata* and potentilla shrubs.

In the rockeries between the lane and the house, she grows a harmonious arrangement of hollyhocks, roses, prostrate juniper, speedwell, arabis, bearberry and catmint. She plans the rock plants for height and colour, finding as she gets older that she tends toward mauves, greys and pinks in the garden. Every year, Peggy says, she intends to plan gardens in February, "but I find I can't do it until I get out there."

Gardening, for Peggy Harvey, is "all-consuming. It's what I do, for hours and hours for most of the year." From April to June she's involved in intense gardening, in July and August she enjoys the results — "My house suffers from it in the summer" — and in the fall she's tidying up and putting away. "In my leisure time, if I can garden, that's what I do."

CHAPTER 6

Short Season

Most gardeners at cottages on the Precambrian Shield find they have a shorter season than gardeners enjoy in Southern Ontario. The weather influences the length of season, but so do the choices gardeners make about how much time they spend at the cottage.

Some families only get up to the cottage on weekends and perhaps a few weeks or one month during the summer. So they concentrate their efforts on having flowers in bloom at a specific time. They resign themselves to starting later and finishing earlier in the garden. Glen Lumis, professor of landscape horticulture at the University of Guelph, says short season has no effect on the types of woody and herbaceous perennials suitable for the cottage garden. The key to choosing appropriate plants rests with their winter hardiness. Consulting a plant-hardiness zone map and finding out the hardiness of ornamental plants before you buy will save effort and money. Most cottages in this book fall within Zone 5 or 4. Information on the growing season can also help determine which vegetable, fruit and berry crops will reach maturity, when to sow seed and when to put out annuals. Frost-free times and the period in which temperatures favour growth determine the growing season.

ABOVE: *Tall cleome, grasses and starry nicotiana, planted in June, provide colour through the short season.*

AT LEFT: *Ground covers such as bergenia, lower right, line the path from boathouse to cottage.*

For frost-free days, the influence of the lakes is important, says meteorologist Terry Gillespie of the University of Guelph. Cold water warms up more slowly than land, so proximity to a lake delays the arrival of spring. As you drive toward Georgian Bay you will find apple trees budding out earlier in the Beaver Valley than near the lakeshore. Large bodies of water take in and store heat in the summer and release it in the autumn and winter. In autumn the warm water delays cold fronts, protecting plants from frost. The southern and eastern shores of Georgian Bay can show differences of more than ten days of frost-free time within 10 miles (16 km) of shore. Cottagers who look forward to one Muskoka farmer's corn, grown only a ten-minute drive from the lake, are surprised some years to find the crop over by the fourth week of August, thanks to a frost that didn't touch lakeside properties.

Elevation also makes a difference to frost-free time. One cottage garden at the same latitude as another might experience frost earlier because high ground gets colder. On the high elevation in Algonquin Park there are only 90 mean annual frost-free days in contrast to 110 at Sudbury. The slope of the ground and degree of shade also control energy. Southern slopes are warmer than northern. By day, valleys are warmest and hilltops coolest; at night, valleys host more frost than hills do.

From year to year, the dates of the first and last frosts will vary: if the mean frost date is May 20, the chance of a frost occurring a week later is one in four. The ability of plants to withstand a light frost depends on the kind of plants, previous weather, how fast the temperature changes, and how long the freeze lasts.

Plant growth depends not only on the length of the growing season but also on the amount of heat available. Most ornamental plants will start growing when the mean daily temperature rises above 42°F. (5.5°C).

On the east shore of Georgian Bay, from around Pointe-au-Baril south to the west side of the Muskoka Lakes gardeners can expect an annual mean growing season of 200 days. Yet gardeners at and to the east of the Muskoka Lakes, in southern Haliburton and southeast in an arc to the northern end of the Kawartha Lakes will experience a mean growing season of 190 days. The northwest part of Haliburton and the western chunk of Algonquin Park have just 180 days.

Fall planting in Zones 5b and 4 needs to be done in late August or early September, at least a month before the deadline in Southern Ontario. In the latter part of the season, plants begin to sense cool nights and set buds; this acclimatization occurs earlier in cottage areas. So that root growth can take place in the new location, fall planting must take place at least a month before the soil gets too cold for growth.

Most gardeners like to push the season, some taking a chance by planting early, others by creating microclimates that are more temperate than the zone would indicate. Walled gardens, for example, capture heat in the south-facing stones and release it at night. Cement foundations accomplish the same heat exchange as do rock walls and the natural outcroppings of the Precambrian Shield. Properly situated, they can also protect a garden from the coldest winds that blow from the northwest and north.

Soil can be warmed earlier by using clear plastic mulches, but the light that comes through encourages weed growth in the moist warm spaces. Coloured plastic is a better choice. Straw mulch, by contrast, will slow down the arrival of heat in the spring.

In a favourable microclimate, gardeners can both grow plants that do not normally grow in that zone and extend the length of the gardening season at the cottage.

❧ July at Georgian Bay ❧

Smooth, wide ripples of granite roll out in front of a Georgian Bay cottage as if the wake of a sea creature had petrified one calm day in prehistory. In between the rock swells rise masses of bright flowers chosen particularly to bloom in July.

Jennifer and Stephen Dattels spend from mid-June to the end of July on Mille Roches Island, so they want as much colour as possible at that time. Because it's a short season, Jennifer doesn't grow early perennials. She has iris but never sees it bloom. Instead she fills the spaces in the rocks with flowers that are glorious by mid-summer - daylilies, tiger lilies, rudbeckia, blanketflowers, evening primrose, white phystigia, dephiniums and Maltese cross. She confesses that black-eyed Susans, ox-eye daisies and coreopsis were dug out of roadside ditches, on the theory that if they could survive there, they could take the rigours of cottage life.

She supplements these perennials with annuals as available, such as petunias and verbena, but grows nothing from seed, as they wouldn't bloom in time for the July garden. Nearer the cottage in the shade of a pine, containers are hidden under an umbrella of impatiens cascading over boulders.

A wild rose transplanted from a boggy place beyond the cottage blooms profusely at a showcase spot beside the path approaching the porch. The garden is ideally sited for easy maintenance and enjoyment. You can

The ripple rocks of Georgian Bay form appealing beds for annuals and perennials and wild seeds that arrive on the wind.

see it from the screened porch and you pass through it on the path, which branches down to the swimming area and over to her parents' cottage.

Jennifer's love of gardening started at the first Mille Roches cottage, where her parents, Frances and Bill Robb, nurtured an attractive garden starting in the early '60s. When the cottage that became the Dattels' was built in 1973, Jennifer started gardening right away. Living in an apartment at the time, she had no city garden, and was delighted when her parents shared transplants, particularly from their lily bed. Now she finds herself with "too many gardens," including a prize-winning city garden and a large enterprise at another country home.

Her husband, Stephen, brought up with a formal perennial garden at his parents' home, shares her enthusiasm. With no landscaper to call on, he enjoys the challenge of gardening at the cottage.

To fill the rocky crevices a foot deep, the Dattels brought in soil, bags at a time, mixing it with manure and peat in search of the perfect pH level. Poor drainage remains a problem; when water hits bedrock, it has nowhere to go. Jennifer has found that sedums do well in little soil on the rock. She has six varieties, as well as hen and chickens. Moss also transplants beautifully and needs hardly any soil.

She has also found lilies most successful, whether or not anyone is around to water them. Indeed,

In view from the paths and the porch and designed for easy maintenance, this garden peaks in July when the owners take holidays.

Jennifer says, they have to rely on Mother Nature when they're not at the cottage. Plants that don't survive the elements aren't attempted a second time. Asked for advice for novice gardeners, she says, "Don't expect it all to happen the first year."

Wind is a constant problem. Surprisingly, Jennifer finds delphiniums wind-resistant if they are well staked. On the positive side, many plants "arrived on their own," some via the wind, including an attractive wild grass with a rounded seedhead that found a home in the ripple rock garden. In the same garden, a milkweed attracts Monarch larvae to its leaves. Jennifer has never used insecticide and the garden has never struggled with an insect problem. Nor is her cottage garden invaded by the weeds that are omnipresent in city gardens.

If the wind shears off some blooms, she moves them indoors for a table arrangement, a move that's perfectly in keeping with this attractive and practical garden, focussed on a short season.

❧ Each Weekend a Changed Garden ❧

Each weekend when the Farrows arrive at their cottage at Stony Lake, the garden has changed from the weekend before.

It's a plus for weekend gardeners, Jill Farrow affirms, discovering what's come up, what's in bloom, variations in the colour range. "Two weeks ago," Grant Farrow observes, "this was a white garden, now it's yellow."

Ice binds their island until on average the third week in April, so on fine spring days when any perennial gardener in the city would be out digging and dividing, the season hasn't even begun for the Farrows. "The crocuses are here the first weekend we can get up, with snow around and bits of ice on the edges," Grant says. Then come the trilliums — "a marvellous show" — lily of the valley, spring tulips and daffodils. Marsh marigolds form a golden horseshoe around an inlet.

Except for an August vacation, the Farrows' gardening is limited to weekends. Even then, they're busy boating, connecting with friends — Jill has been coming to the cottage since she was fifteen — and volunteering. "Any perennial gardener would do more," she says.

Nevertheless, the attention lavished on this garden is obvious. Bergenia, ivy and hosta and *Aegopodium* shimmer in the shade beside the path leading up from the boathouse. The *Aegopodium* (Jill calls it Bishop's mantle, or goutweed) gleams at night, illuminating the path.

Outside the cottage door, ivy twines out of a Stony Lake turtle shell.

Weekend gardeners look forward to discovering what's in bloom as they arrive at the cottage. Here a cosmos shines in the sun.

A night-blooming clematis, delphiniums and cleome benefit from windbreak provided by the building. Wind is a major factor in dessicating the plants, but it does keep mosquitoes and black-flies away.

Most weekends, meals are taken on a patio that affords the best view of the gardens bordering the path that curves invitingly along the centre of the island. For the perennial beds, Grant laid logs in triangles to hold the soil, which is brought to the island by barge and moved up from the lake by wheelbarrow.

On one side, yarrow, pink coneflower, cosmos, a cranesbill (*Geranium endressii* Johnson's Blue), creeping Jenny and wild daisy have been established with perennial blue salvia, which Jill cuts back to encourage a second bloom.

On the other side, she planted annual zinnias and nicotiana with a peony, juniper, coral bells and a blue hydrangea. A bench pew provides a resting spot.

Further along, lavender, coral bells, artemisia, a pale purple bergamot, blue lupines, white gloriosa daisies, veronicas, Blue Clips campanula and lilies continue the blue-and-pink palette, with lady's mantle bestowing a froth of pale green.

Jill Farrow feels strongly about what should be grown at the cottage. Although not a totally natural landscape, "the whole range of daisies is appropriate, and all the wildflowers, and plants the early people used to grow — delphiniums, peony, foxgloves, lilacs."

A path curves through perennial beds at Stony Lake.

Certainly plants that like sharp drainage do well, says Jill, a member of the Garden Club of Toronto and a board member of the Royal Botanical Gardens.

The central path leads between other beds of artemisia, sunflowers, liatris, phlox and zinnias and goldenrod, sumac, coneflowers, peony, yarrow, hosta, a huge clump of veronica, and heliopsis, also called false sunflower. One patch of hot colour boasts phlox, white gloriosa daisies, peonies, lupines and red bergamot. With iris and phlox, Jill planted valerian. Its tall stems can reach 4 feet (1.2 m), producing fragrant flowers mid- to late-summer.

Jill muses that a real challenge for gardeners is marking the location of perennials so they won't be damaged before they come up in the spring when the gardener is cultivating — plastic markers look tacky, metal ones may spoil the look of the flower bed. She likes the example of one gardener of her acquaintance who writes the botanical names on small rocks. She's delighted with anise hyssop (*Agastache anethedora*), sometimes called licorice mint, a gift from a friend. Friends in the old Stony Lake community "trade and share and do all kinds of things back and forth." A red bergamot was another gift.

Further along, where the original house on the island burned down some years ago, a flat grassy area has become a croquet lawn. Each summer the Farrows offer the Stony Lake Annual International Invitational Croquet Tournament, the international component arriving in the form of some of Grant Farrow's colleagues. Women don long white tea dresses, men sport straw boaters, and Grant serves Pimm's from a lined cement mixer. The trickiest part of the tournament may be manoeuvring around the lilac bushes that have naturalized in the lawn.

As most of the island's natural habitat has been left undisturbed, the Farrows have the opportunity to observe a wide variety of animal inhabitants. Jill and Grant know where to find flimsy loon nests on the exposed rocky shore, and also welcome a large population of turtles that clamber up a stony slope to lay eggs. Beaver can be a problem, even chewing two-by-fours, and deer walk over the ice in winter.

But "the varmint most mischievous to us in many years," says Grant ruefully, "was the vole." Voles were the varmints that chewed around the base of junipers until they fell over. However, after one summer with a particularly high vole population, the next year they were less in evidence. The Farrows speculate that mink may have gone after them.

Jill uses bonemeal and a granular 20-20-20 fertilizer when she plants and adds nothing thereafter, but says they are working on a more natural approach. Out of an old cedar dock, Grant constructed a four-bin composter next to a heap of soil and sand. They are beginning to mulch garden beds with compost on weekends in fall and spring.

Regardless of the gardening chores they assign themselves, the Farrows keenly anticipate the changes awaiting them each weekend in their alluring garden at Stony Lake.

❦ EXTENDING THE SEASON ❦

When frost is predicted for Muskoka — often as early as late August — Suzann Partridge hauls out plastic sheeting.

She has spectacular gardens to protect — two large vegetable plots bordered by shrubs and flowers, a herb garden and a new strawberry patch. In the more than twenty years since she and husband Jon settled on a former farm off South Monck Drive near Bracebridge, gardening has become her passion. But there's an extra incentive to keep frost at bay a few more weeks. On the last weekend in September, visitors on the Muskoka autumn studio tour pour into the farm by car and bus to see Jon Partridge's pottery. The gardens, frost permitting, are a bonus.

A gravel path with a perennial border to the right leads to the studio. In midsummer the border boasts hollyhocks, cleome, hydrangea, hostas, tansey, orange cosmos, five heritage roses, gloriosa daisies, ajuga, pinks, columbine, two kinds of monkshood, peonies, liatris, beebalm, silver-cup lavatera, and delphiniums.

The vegetable garden in front of the studio is guarded by a scarecrow with a black bird face — clay covered with metallic oxide — and wings fashioned from black garbage bags cut into fearsome fringes. In this area, Partridge grows beans, beets, tomatoes, cucumbers, peas, potatoes, cabbages, onions and squash. She is a regular entrant — and winner — at the local fall fair with her vegetables. Sunflowers tower near the corn and anywhere else birds have dropped seeds.

In a herb garden beside the showroom, a huge clump of borage (*Borago officialis*), a starry blue-flowered herb good in drinks and salads, seeds itself among other herbs and edible flowers. Rosemary, lavender, bay leaf, thyme, dill, chives, catnip, sage, parsley, fennel, feverfew, basil and sweet Cicely (*Myrrhis odorata*) lend a fine aroma to the air. Several kinds of mint are contained in barrels. The tender herbs grow in pots sunk into the ground. Hops twine up the showroom wall.

On the far side of the showroom is the strawberry patch, in which the runners go almost unnoticed beside gourds and a new introduction — orange-blooming Mexican sunflowers. Suzann and neighbour Lyette Beaulac, a weaver, often go together to buy exotic seeds from catalogues. These sunflowers were one of their experiments a few summers ago.

Suzann says she's now obsessive about gardening: "I go to bed with seed catalogues." Local craftswoman Tina Chambers admires the garden so much she has designed a sweater called "Suzann's Gardens." But there was a time when the Partridges knew nothing about gardening. Their first vegetable patch was planted in part of a field that a neighbour had plowed. Twitchgrass choked that crop. She recalls going out to the garden, son Clayton on her hip, and puzzling over a tall plant. Pulled up, it revealed itself as a radish gone to seed.

"When we first got the place, the weeds were up to our chests." And each year the weather varied; "There were years of drought. We have had frost in June and in the middle of August and snow at the end of May. . . . Each year I learned a lot."

The next vegetable garden was located where logs of the original barn lay rotting and chickens once scratched in the barnyard. The combination made a rich soil, naturally composted. In that garden now she grows thornless raspberry canes, carrots, beets, spinach, rutabagas, parsnips, three kinds of lettuce, garlic, climbing peas, basil, summer savory, fennel and coriander. Horseradish is grown in a pot to contain voracious roots. She recommends tomatilloes — husk-covered fruits akin to tomatoes — for salsa. Asparagus, yielding 3 or 4 pounds (1–2 kg) in each of six pickings, is a special treat in the spring in Muskoka, where until recently fresh produce was not plentiful.

Suzann plants intensively to keep down weeds and organizes companion plantings such as marigolds near cabbages to discourage bugs. The only dust she uses is dinosaur fossil dust she and Lyette ordered from an organic gardening magazine to use against Colorado potato bugs and other leaf-eating insects. In rainy weather it washes off, and Suzann, with so many other things on the go, can't keep up with the dusting, so in some years her potato plants look "like skeletons."

The nearby flower garden is at its best in July because of the Asiatic lilies, according to Suzann, but it also contains purple coneflowers, poppies sown from seed, artemisia, hen and chickens, Jacob's ladder, pearly everlasting, black-eyed Susans, foxglove, veronicas, helianthus, deep purple Canterbury bells, and in the spring, Siberian iris and violets.

Although deer and even a moose have been sighted elsewhere on the farm, they tend to stay in their natural browsing areas. But there have been problems with domestic animals. A neighbour who had been sheltering a rabbit from the winter in a garage phoned one day in a panic — a weasel was getting in. So Suzann put the rabbit in with her chickens. Come spring, despite clover in the grass, the bunny was helping itself to emerging vegetable leaves. Suzann is hoping to find it a new home. Recently she acquired a large puppy that accompanies her out in the garden: "While I was deadheading, she was flattening."

Although the soil a few miles away may be sandy, at this location it's pure clay, she says. With runoff and the plants taking up the nutrients, "I have to keep putting in humus." She keeps two composters on the go as well as a "huge area behind the shed," and rototills the compost into the garden, adding leaves every year. Peat from the swamp goes onto the gardens every other year, and she uses horse manure, although it comes complete with weed seeds.

When her son and daughter Shannon were younger, she insisted they help with the weeding. Now they're in their twenties, and she's the main gardener, with Jon lending a hand when she needs it to place railroad ties or put up a pea fence.

Tender perennials such as begonias and geraniums are planted in Jon's pots and taken into his studio for the winter where they bask in humidity and light from large windows. She even keeps impatiens over, including one variety her mother gave her in the 1970s. Cuttings from it are in gardens all over Muskoka and Toronto.

Suzann Partridge relies on frilly ornamental cabbage and kale in green, purple and white to withstand the first fall frost. She believes she was one of the first to grow it in Muskoka back in the '70s. It can be found edging most of the paths where visitors will walk come September.

AT LEFT: *Away from the lake, perennials, herbs and vegetables risk damage from frosts that can strike as early as late August in Muskoka.*

Tuberous begonias add colour to a country home where the owners rely mostly on native plants that survive their absence.

🌿 PLANTING FOR YOUR ABSENCE 🌿

For the time being, the gardening season is short for a couple who make a stone schoolhouse their summer home. So they seek out plants that look after themselves.

Since buying the school in Ufford in Muskoka in 1974, Gilbert and Earlene Sutton have tried growing many plants. Severe winters, frosts as late as June 8, and the necessity in recent years for the couple to be elsewhere in June and in the fall hampered many of their gardening efforts.

They tried an S-shaped shrub bed in the schoolyard, planting snowberry, flowering mock orange and Russian olive, but perhaps because the soil was inhospitable and the wind strong, the shrubs did not survive. Soil at the site was a mixture of sand, where the baseball diamond had been, and clay. The back half of the lot is wet.

The Suttons have seen some elms along the fence-line die, but one has reseeded itself. A row of conifers was growing along the rural roadside, and the Suttons planted many more pines, both for privacy and a noise barrier. As the pines mature and lose their lower branches, the couple is now looking for other trees to fill in the gaps.

"We tried a vegetable garden, quite extensive, fertilized by manure, but we would miss parts of it when in the city or out of the country," says Earlene. " So we have to find ways where things look after themselves. Therefore we [now] have native plants."

The one-room schoolhouse, which dates to 1893 and is one of only two surviving stone schoolhouses in Muskoka, closed in 1965 when a consolidated school opened in the district. For a time the stone school served as a community centre for dances and parties, but it had been empty for a year when the Suttons bought it. It sits at the intersection of a busy rural road and a country lane where a neighbour's sign informs drivers: Blind Goose and Children Playing.

During one sabbatical year, the Suttons lived at the schoolhouse. Earlene, who had joined the Women's Institute, invited members to hold a reunion on the property for former pupils. More than a hundred former students and their families enjoyed an afternoon of old-fashioned races, a picnic and lemonade.

Against a sunny western wall, Earlene Sutton planted a bed of daylilies of many colours, including lemon lilies from her parents' farm. The bees, however, have been busy pollinating and now orange and yellow lilies predominate. In

Orange daylilies are an easy-care choice
for gardeners that need plants to look after themselves.

a border on the south side of the schoolhouse, Earlene planted yellow-flowering *Lysimachia punctata*, lilies, chives, astilbe, small sunflowers, monkshood and Jacob's ladder. Earlene plans to try bleeding heart in her old-fashioned garden next.

Visitors are invited to join them in a game of boules on a grassy septic-tile bed. Since both Suttons enjoy cooking with herbs, dinner might feature dishes flavoured with basil, parsley, thyme and sage picked from containers minutes before.

Trembling aspen that they planted on the east side of the property quickly grew into huge trees, forming a screen that filtered the east sun and made a wonderful rustling sound outside the bedroom they added to the one-room school. As the trees finished their lifespan and were taken down, more light reached the ground, encouraging the growth of woodland plants. Bloodroot, lady's-slipper, trilliums, violets and lily of the valley light up the pine needles in the woodland each spring. The Suttons collect rainwater in a barrel for watering the wildflowers. Some of their wild plants came from a cottage owned by friends on Georgian Bay. A mullein or Indian tobacco has seeded itself. "I'm even transplanting thistles," Earlene says.

In a corner formed by the entrance to the schoolhouse and one stone wall, the Suttons have had great success with Solomon's seal, which has grown to heights of at least 4 feet (1.2 m) and spread widely. The original clump came from a farmhouse in Southern Ontario where Earlene grew up.

When the couple retires and moves to the schoolhouse year-round, they plan to build a shallow pond, taking advantage of the high water-table on the back part of their lot, where marsh grasses now grow. They envisage grasses and water lilies.

"We hope to have a walled garden," Earlene adds. "It will be stone; the west wind is quite strong." They plan to build the stone wall at least 5 feet (1.5 m) high around a space roughly 20 by 30 feet, (6 by 9 m) on the site of their former vegetable garden. They hope the wall will create a favourable microclimate for apples trees, particularly old-fashioned favourites such as Cortland and Spartan. The drainage will need to be improved, Gilbert notes. Both projects will reduce the amount of grass that has to be cut.

The schoolhouse, which had windows "up high, so the children couldn't look out," is a cave, says Gilbert. Even after he extended the windows downward to let in more light from the south, the dwelling still felt like a cave. So he designed a tower, 29 feet (8.5 m) high — shorter than he wanted — but in conformance with building bylaws — which currently is reached from the indoors by a ladder. Windowed on four sides, the tower allows the couple to "appropriate" the view of surrounding fields as part of their Muskoka garden.

🌿 COME SUMMER, CONSTANT BLOOM 🌿

In late summer, a magnificent garden at the head of Lake Rosseau evokes a Muskoka sunset in wide bands of flowers.

Vibrant perennials in white, yellow, gold, orange, pink, coral and crimson punctuated with drifts in deep blue cut a swath across the edge of the top lawn and reappear on the next level down toward the lake. A border outlining the original log cottage, the attached screened porch and open verandah echoes the sunset palette.

Thomas (Tommy) Jarvis cultivates the garden so as to have constant bloom in July, when he and his wife, Mary Louise, and family are at the cottage, and in August, when his brother-in-law, David Kent, and his wife, Mary, are in residence.

Lupines, poppies and columbines, for example, are lovely, but there's no point in

This large-scale setting at the head of Lake Joseph calls for great swaths of tall plants: lilies, liatris, phlox, heliopsis, Shasta daisies and hollyhocks.

planting them if cottagers aren't there to enjoy them in June, Tommy points out.

The thing that's changing in the cottage world, he says, is that fewer people have the luxury of enjoying a lengthy stay at the cottage. At the turn of the century, when his wife's family bought the property for its dramatic view looking down the lake, they used to stay at the cottage from mid-June until mid-September. The next generation did the same. Nowadays, he observes, when young people are working, the higher up the ladder they go, the shorter the vacation they seem able to take at one time.

With a shorter season, cottagers interested in gardening need to focus on plants that bloom during a specified time.

Tommy has tried to convert the garden entirely to flowering

perennials, though he created one beautiful bed of native Solomon's seal and Jack-in-the-pulpit under a pine, and would encourage wild columbine and hepatica if they appeared. But small plants aren't much use on a garden of this scale, he observes. "With a big garden, you have to make a statement."

Work began on the garden about fifteen years ago, starting with transplanting birch saplings from the edge of the woods to sunny points in front of the cottage. Trees were cut down to open the view toward the lake. Then Tommy began planting around rock outcrops on the slope. "The rocks were around — big stones — they were a natural. One of the joys of the Shield is the natural rock formations. Shallow soil on top of it is deep enough to grow flowers successfully."

Mary Louise's aunt, Mrs. Augustus Walker, had grown ferns and junipers and planted peonies on this property. Even though their bloom comes to an end in late June, he has no intention of removing the peonies, now an impressive ninety years old.

As Tommy began expanding the few existing beds and creating extensive new ones, his children helped replace the "hopeless" clay soil with loads of good topsoil.

The property has been tiered into two levels of lawn, with shorter stone staircases winding through the gardens to the next level instead of a precipitous staircase leading down the slope to the lake. Steep rock cliffs at the shoreline are edged in sumac, juniper, oak and elderberry. Stairs descend to a landing at the lake, where steps lead right into the water.

Tommy's interest in flowers came from his father, who was a professor at the Ontario Agricultural College in Guelph. These days, in a greenhouse in the basement at his city home, he plants seeds for the cottage in mid-March or early April. Except for phlox and lilies, he grows all his perennials from seed. He transfers the seedlings to peat pots and takes them to

Lilies, about a thousand in all, are at their prime in July and August when the owners are at the cottage.

the cottage later in the spring. A friend in Rosseau waters the flats and rakes the flower beds. Trying to garden in May or June "you can be eaten alive" by black-flies rising up from the soil, Tommy says. Although he wears a protective mosquito outfit in the spring, he leaves most of the planting until July.

He finds weeding a garden of that size "horrendous," particularly trying to eradicate twitchgrass and vetch, but does some spraying to control the weeds and uses slug bait for the hostas.

He considers the lilies the glory of the garden. Asiatics bloom in late June and July, trumpet lilies in mid-July, and Oriental lilies carry on into September. To get away from the standard orange daylily, he imports different hues from a Missouri company. Both lilies and daylilies grow and multiply in every kind of soil. "They do flourish, I must have a thousand of them."

Daylilies and hosta are the backbone of this garden, colourful and requiring little or no work. Shasta daisies providing white contrast are a vital part of the garden in July, and phlox in a coral hue are "the most beautiful August flower."

Tommy has recently been replacing orange daylilies near the carport with phlox, deep red lilies and balloonflower (*Platycodon*) and is working on a new bed to the right of the carport. Purple liatris, blue veronica, lilies in peach, phlox, white campanula and Shasta daisies, black-eyed Susans, gloriosa daisies, veronica and heliopsis grow with single hollyhocks of deep pink and crimson, some of them reaching

7 feet (2 m). Hollyhocks being a biennial, next year's plants are grown in a small nursery bed.

In the border around the cottage, Oriental lilies, mauve phlox, gloriosa daisies, heliopsis, hosta, pink and yellow lilies, phlox, and others grow; a white freckled lily reigns at one corner.

Hummingbirds whirr in the garden at the edge of the first lawn, where myriad perennials bloom on either side of a stone staircase, among them sundrops, black-eyed Susans, white and pink lilies, yarrow, yellow coreopsis, lady's mantle, pink phlox, baby's breath, Stoke's aster (*Stokesia*), gloriosa daisies, purple coneflower and purple globe thistle. Creeping phlox and sedum edge this garden at the lower lawn.

One problem, notes Tommy, is preventing yellow-toned flowers from taking over the colour scheme. For that reason, he keeps weeding out gloriosa daisies.

In an area near the pumphouse steps, he's growing a carpet of periwinkle and replacing daylilies with Asiatics. In another planting, the white spires of obedient plant and feathery astilbe make a fine late August show among juniper; another bed holds purple beebalm growing near yellow yarrow, and purple and peach lilies, anchored by large boulders.

Like many gardeners, Tommy Jarvis claims he's "never completely happy" with his garden. But his selection of plants that flourish in Muskoka at the height of the summer provides a perfect example for gardeners who are limited to a short season at the cottage.

✿ PLANTS RESCUED AND TRADED ✿

A Lake Rosseau cottager has created a remarkable garden without buying a single plant. Gardening almost entirely in July and August — the family goes to the cottage only the odd weekend in spring and fall — Brenda Yates grows flowers from seed, trades with friends and rescues plants doomed to destruction.

"I refuse to buy them," she says with a smile. "Rescuing plants is so exciting."

Across the bay, for example, a derelict farmhouse was about to be sold. Brenda took samples of the flowering plants, including wild pink roses "like powder puffs." Not long afterward, bulldozers destroyed the remaining plants. Behind an old store in Port Carling where graders were at work, Brenda rescued several peonies. Single hollyhocks came from another threatened site.

If she is at a friend's garden and sees something "different," Brenda will ask if she can trade. Recently she gave some bergamot (*Monarda didyma*) in exchange for a light green, dark green hosta for her growing hosta collection, which includes the bluish "elephant ears," variegated green on white and white on green.

She also shares plants with other cottagers. "If anybody new comes into the area, for a bread-and-butter present I take some plants in a basket."

As she gives a tour of the garden in August, she frequently stops to take a seedhead and scatter the seeds in the flower beds. If a plant fails to thrive in one location, Brenda will give it another chance in a different spot, perhaps the other side of the plot. But if, in the end, "Nature doesn't want that, Nature has to have a say."

Flowers such as phlox, artemisia and black-eyed Susans are grown from seed, traded or rescued from abandoned gardens.

An active member of the Garden Club of Hamilton, Brenda brushes aside the term knowledgeable, but agrees that with experience, "the hours and the years," a gardener learns what works at the cottage and what doesn't.

When a friend tried clematis in Muskoka, Brenda cautioned her that it would not likely survive. "In the end you have to admit defeat," she says, for some exotic plants. "I need to garden in a way my gardens will be sustaining if I do have to go down to the city."

Brenda also aims to have colour in the garden from spring until fall, even if she isn't there to enjoy it. Lilacs and daffodils in front of the cottage and all through the woods give way to the colourful daisylike plants that light up the summer, ending with hardy mums along a pathway in the fall.

When Terry and Brenda Yates brought their property, not far from the Joe River, they were delighted to learn from neighbours that it had once been the site of the Gregory Hotel, which burned down in 1968. Terry points out a crib from the hotel dock, where steamboats used to pick up mail from the Gregory post office. The Yates hope one day to encounter people who used to stay at the hotel and learn more of its history.

"The original hotel would have had some flowers," Brenda observes. Lilacs have spread in a band between the former hotel and the lake, a flowering tree survives from that era and she is "still splitting rhubarb" from one clump that perhaps gave the guests rhubarb pie. "We pick wild strawberries and mix them with rhubarb."

The garden was fairly overgrown by the time the Yates moved in, "but as I was rooting around, I found irises, black-eyed Susans and some phlox — it was a matter, again, of saving them." She says she began planting first by a walkway that had been built by the previous owners. Between the house and the lake, she grows vinca, hosta, tansy, the rescued peonies and roses, medium purple iris, lemon lilies, and harebells, some blue, some white.

By the boathouse, violets and bright pink creeping phlox announce spring. They are followed by summer flowers — yellow evening primrose, black-freckled tiger lilies, black-eyed Susans, the yellow and orange of blanket flower, mauve, phlox, yellow foxglove, lupine, purple liatris and grey artemisia.

Brenda tries to work with the soil on the property, every so often adding compost. "I think most of our cottagers are composting now. It sure saves on the garbage."

Brenda attempted vegetable gardening at the cottage once years ago — tomatoes, carrots, beans — but soon found that rabbits made short work of the produce, taking one bite out of each of the tomatoes, for example.

In the sunny lawn at the entrance to the cottage, the Yates planted a white pine in honour of the birth of each grandchild. When Kirsten, Jessica, Alaina and Amanda were small, they put a footprint and handprint under their names in cement markers at the base of their trees. Little Adam will soon be adding his prints under a young pine.

Across the driveway, a garden of evening primrose blooms within a circle of tree trunks. Brenda says they couldn't move the stump and the pieces of trunk so they made a garden. A plaster dwarf adds a whimsical touch.

In a south garden beside the cottage, Brenda has planted the herb burnet (*Sanguisorba minor*). For people who can't digest cucumber, burnet, with its cucumber taste, makes a perfect substitute in a salad, she suggests. It grows in a bed with black-eyed Susans, veronica, lemon lilies, lupines — the seed came from roadsides in Newfoundland — obedient plant, coneflowers, coreopsis, gaillardia and sweet peas.

To catch the full effect of the sweet peas, you have to be inside the cottage. In two bedrooms, windows are thrown open early in the summer, allowing the sweet peas to twine up the screens. Extending the sight and scent of sweet peas and the hum of bees within makes the most of a summer garden in a season that's all too short.

🌿 GARDENING FOR THE BIG DAY 🌿

As cool, wet weather seeped through June and into July, Caley Taylor wasn't asking for a miracle A not sun, light breezes or warmth, just no rain for one special day.

On July 20, 1996, two hundred guests would arrive at the Taylor cottage on Lake Joseph to celebrate daughter Robin's wedding to Todd, known as Toby, Schertzer.

Robin and Toby became engaged the week after the big July windstorm in 1995. Unfazed by the potential for errant weather, Caley Taylor immediately began planning a wedding in the style of a Muskoka garden party. "I really felt this was the best spot for it," Caley said. "They met in Muskoka and they have spent so much time here, it's the perfect place for them."

The bride would walk down a path from the cottage to the dock, passing under a birch arbour constructed by her father, Tony. The growing season, behind by at least two weeks, meant that sweet peas planted to twine up the arbor had reached only knee height. The resourceful mother of the bride would weave cedar boughs around the arbour.

After the ceremony on the dock, the reception would take place in a tent at a nearby Taylor property along the shoreline. "I'll be carting over, I guess, all told, a hundred and fifty planters," Caley

Dried grass tumbles out of a fishing creel on a log outbuilding at Lake Joseph.

explained the week before the wedding. In June she had planted these containers with herbs, perennials, miniature roses, grasses and annuals, no two alike. Some would become centrepieces; large terra-cotta pots would create a bower in the tent.

She chose a soft palette of pink, blue, purple and white, with touches of yellow. But in some planters "a surprise cosmos" bloomed in vivid orange, the one colour she didn't want. Caley pulled out a few, then laughed and left the rest.

Ten days before the event, it became obvious that dull weather was slowing down the plants. So most of the 150 containers were trundled from the cottage patio down to the dock for more sun.

Caley undertakes a prodigious effort in container gardening at the cottage every summer. As well as tending perennials in beds, "pockets in rocks" and anywhere she can find a few inches of soil, she regularly plants at least 125 containers. She finds the planting season several weeks behind that of Toronto, not only because of the threat of frost. "It's almost better to wait a week or two after the twenty-fourth of May. Until then the ground is so cool the plants don't do anything." But once the ground warms up, sometimes as late as mid-June, plants "take off" and will look great until the end of September.

One of the biggest challenges for cottagers comes with being a weekend gardener, Caley recalls. She advises deadheading and pinching back plants at the end of each weekend to encourage more bloom. Once her children were old enough to leave at home, she began taking a week in June just for planting. The household includes Kari, Kristi, Ryan, two dogs and six cats. Caley often wondered what she would do if the young people wanted summer jobs in the city, but fortunately all found or invented jobs in Muskoka.

The Taylors bought their property in 1974, siting the cottage in a clearing according to stone pathways in place since the turn of the century. At the rear of the house, Caley empties her planters every fall, building up a rich bed of soil on rock rubble left after blasting for the foundation.

Periwinkle was growing on the property, and Caley moves it around. Taking a wagon and spade, she also transplants ferns, violets, daisies and sweet woodruff to gardens near the house. Around the cottage she grows astilbe, coreopsis, lythrum, cranesbill geranium, perennial sunflowers and veronica, lady's mantle and foxglove. For anyone looking for easy plants that spread quickly, she recommends mint and tansy — "it can grow in the crummiest soil."

Caley prepares beds and planters ahead of planting time, bringing in bags of soil, more expensive but more convenient than a truckload, especially when soil has to be carried to planters on top of the boathouse. She adds compost in the spring and top-dresses beds, borders and planters with sheep manure. "I don't like digging up perennials. I don't want to disturb them. When I'm putting in additional plants, I dig holes for them and pull out any tree roots, which you get even in raised beds."

Some of the 150 containers planted for a wedding hold
herbs, perennials, miniature roses, grasses and annuals —
no two arrangements alike.

On either side of an arbour leading to the cottage, perennial sweet peas, morning glory, cleome, and nicotiana form a colourful entrance to a stone patio etched in thyme.

Caley says she's learned from experience and books, and gets help from knowledgeable friends and her sister, Barbara Waite. Taking the advice of one gardening friend, she usually places three plants in one hole for a look that's instantly lush.

Naturalized yellow sedum spreads a thick carpet over a rock outcrop at the northeast side of the cottage. "If anything wants to seed itself, that's fine," she says. "I want my garden to look part of the landscape." She lets grasses grow within and outside the small rock borders of perennial beds, achieving a harmonious blending of wild and cultivated.

Caley has amassed an amazing collection of containers. "A lot of people who have worked around the place bring me old things they know I will like." At one time a hotel stood on the property and cast-offs were pitched into the bush — cooking pots, kettles, pans. It doesn't matter if the bottoms have rusted out, "as long as it has sides I plant it." In one kettle she planted chamomile.

She makes use of baskets, tureens, and on her dock, huge terra-cotta planters and half barrels. One cast-iron pot with no drainage holes has become a home for plants dug up in the swamp, but most containers do need drainage holes. For those without, she finds herself out in her nightie in an overnight shower dragging them to the shelter of a shed roof.

In one planter, she concentrated on herbs — chives, dill, lemon balm and ivy. In another she planted ivy, red, white and pink nicotiana and purslane (*Portulaca oleracea sativa*). "I smack 'em full, even when they're first planted." A wooden drawer from an old icehouse holds impatiens. Elsewhere, morning glories twine up the chains holding a black iron pot. In one half barrel on the dock a pine tree seeded itself and is now growing out of a hole in the barrel.

Wind is a problem, especially on the dock. As a support, "birch twigs are wonderful to put in planters, if you're smart, when you plant." In several containers she uses birch saplings cut down by an Ontario Hydro crew as a tall support for sunflowers and grasses, planted with licorice plant, gerbera and thistles. She sticks the saplings in the middle in a pyramid and ties them together with raffia.

Caley has never liked draceana in containers, preferring tall grasses such as Foerster's reed grass (*Calamagrostis* Karl Foerster), northern sea oats (*Chasmanthum latifolium*) and the old-fashioned ribbon grass (*Phalaris arundinacea* Picta). She might combine grass with dusty miller and pink impatiens, creeping baby's breath and hen and chickens. She leaves the grasses in containers all winter, taking them out in the spring when dried to use in decoration. One plump, honey-coloured bunch looks like a horse's tail springing out of a creel on the wall of a wooden outbuilding.

One spring, a mallard made a nest of the grasses in a container. For nearly a month, she sat on eight eggs while Caley checked twice a day hoping to catch a glimpse of the ducklings. But one afternoon, seven out of the eight hatched and mother and ducklings departed before Caley could see them.

In a wooden building sat the 200 small terra-cotta pots that Caley Taylor was decorating individually for the guests with birchbark, dried grasses, seedheads, dried chives, daylily pods, nigella, maple seeds, cones, dried flowers, all gathered around the cottage, all tied with raffia. Each pot would contain a dark green candle. "We're not looking at elegant," Caley said. "We're using the natural. I always gather stuff. . . . I use a lot at Christmas in arrangements."

On the Thursday before the wedding, it began to rain and carried on for twelve hours. On the wedding day, breezes were brisk, the weather cool. The sun shone all day.

Sedum, violets, lilies, coreopsis, coneflowers, and beebalm are all plants recommended for cottages by experienced gardeners.

CHAPTER 7

Recommended Plants

On a November day when the wind is dancing the jive with fallen leaves in the backyard, it's delicious to sit inside revisiting the gardens of summer. Voices of the gardeners in this book murmur into the daydream. "*Corydalis lutea*, the only perennial that blooms all summer in shade or sun . . . A cottage garden shouldn't be a formal garden . . . Beebalm is very satisfactory . . . Nothing bothers the sedum . . . You can buy Asiatic lilies in varieties that will bloom successively through July and August . . . Campanulas are an excellent group of plants for the cottage . . . The ferns up here are a real standby . . . Do you know the balloonflower?"

Of the plants in the following list, some showed up in one garden after another, indicating that they are well suited visually and relatively easy to maintain at a cottage. Some of the less popular came highly recommended. Dozens more could have been included. Most gardens in this book fall into plant-hardiness Zones 5 and 4, but many plants listed, particularly the shrubs and roses, are hardy in lower zones.

There is a mix of native plants and cultivars. Ferns can serve as ground cover, or as accent or background in a shade garden. An effort was made to exclude plants that are invasive and could spread and choke native growth. The Muskoka Heritage Foundation recommended some plants. And some I have grown myself, suggesting that just about anyone should have luck with them.

GROUND COVERS

Arctostaphylos uva-ursi (Bearberry)
Asarum canadense (Wild ginger)
Aster macrophyllus (Bigleaf aster)
Cornus canadensis (Bunchberry)
Dianthus deltoides (Maiden pink)
Ferns
Fragari virginiana (Wild strawberry)
Gaultheria procumbens (Wintergreen)
Galium triflorum (Scented bedstraw)
Mitchella repens (Partridgeberry)
Nepeta mussinii (Persian catmint)
Phlox subulata (Moss phlox)
Sedum (Stonecrop)
Thymus (Thyme)
Trifolium repens (White clover)
Vaccinium angustifolium (Lowbush blueberry)

MEADOW

Agastache foeniculum (Blue giant hyssop)
Asclepias tuberosa (Butterfly weed)
Aster novae-angliae (New England aster)
Aquilegia canadensis (Wild columbine)
Coreopsis lanceolata (Lance-leaved coreopsis)
Echinacea purpurea (Purple coneflower)
Geum triflorum (Prairie smoke)
Helianthus (Sunflower)
Liatris spicata (Gayfeather)
Lupinus (Lupine)
Monarda fistulosa (Wild bergamot)
Oenothera biennis (Evening primrose)
Physostegia virginiana (Obedient plant)
Rudbeckia hirta (Black-eyed Susan)
Sisyrinchium montanum (Blue-eyed grass)
Verbena hastata (Blue vervain)

PERENNIALS AND BULBS IN SUN

Campanula (Bellflower)
Coreopsis lanceolata (Lance-leaved coreopsis)
Echinacea purpurea (Purple coneflower)
Echinops (Globe thistle)
Geranium (Cranesbill)
Heuchera sanguinea (Coral bells)
Helenium autumnale (Sneezeweed)
Helianthus (Sunflower)
Heliopsis (False sunflower)
Hemerocallis (Daylilies)
Liatris (Gayfeather)
Lilium (Lilies)
Monarda didyma (Beebalm, bergamot)
Monarda fistulosa (Wild bergamot)
Penstamon (Beardtongue)
Phlox (Phlox)
Platycodon (Balloonflower)
Polemonium reptans (Jacob's ladder)
Rudbeckia fulgida sullivantii Goldsturm
   (Goldsturm black-eyed Susan)
Salvia (Salvia)
Sidalcea (Sidalcea or Mallow)
Stokesia (Stoke's aster)
Veronica (Speedwell)

FOR SHADE

Aconitum (Monkshood)
Alchemilla mollis (Lady's mantle)
Astilbe (Astilbe)
Bergenia cordifolia (Heartleaf bergenia, Saxifrage)
Cimicifuga racemosa (Snakeroot)
Corydalis lutea (Yellow corydalis)
Dicentra cucularia (Dutchman's breeches)
Dicentra eximia (Fringed bleeding heart)

Dicentra spectabilis (Bleeding heart)
Ferns
Heuchera sanguinea (Coral bells)
Hosta (Plantain lily)
Geranium (Cranesbill)
Lamium (Dead nettle)
Polygonatum biflorum (Solomon's seal)
Pulmonaria (Lungwort)
Tiarella cordifolia (Foamflower)

SHRUBS

Caragana arborescens (Siberian pea shrub)
Cornus stolonifera (Red-osier dogwood)
Physocarpus opulifolius (Ninebark)
Potentilla fruticosa (Shrubby Potentilla or Cinquefoil)
Prunus virginiana (Choke cherry)
Sambucus canadensis (Elderberry)
Spirea bumalda Anthony Waterer (Anthony Waterer spirea)
Spirea bumalda Froebelli (Froebel's spirea)
Symphoricarpos albus (Snowberry)
Viburnum cassinoides (Wild raisin)
Viburnum lentago (Nannyberry)
Viburnum trilobum (High-bush cranberry)

Roses
CLIMBERS: Henry Kelsey, John Cabot, William Baffin
TALL SHRUBS: Alexander Mackenzie, John Davis, Scabrosa,
Thérèse Bugnet, Martin Frobisher, Jens Munk
LOW SHRUBS: Champlain, Henry Hudson, David Thompson,
Charles Albanel, Louis Jolliet

WETLANDS

Caltha palustris (Marsh marigold)
Chelone glabra (White turtlehead)
Eupatorium maculatum (Spotted Joe-Pye-weed)
Gentiana andrewsii (Bottle or closed gentian)
Iris versicolor (Blue flag)
Lobelia cardinalis (Cardinal flower)
Mentha arvensis (Wild mint)
Salix discolor (Pussywillow)
Thalictrum polygamum (Tall meadow rue)

❧ Acknowledgments ❧

For contacts and research, the author thanks Stephen Booth; Susan Biggar; Bonnie Bergsma, botanist; Elizabeth Bryce; Gayle Carlyle of the Muskoka Heritage Foundation; Sheila Corkill; Jill Farrow; the Garden Club of Toronto; Terry Gillespie, meteorologist, Land Resource Science, the University of Guelph; Anne Hertzberg; Mary Hincks; Christine Hughes; Henry Kock, horticultural interpreter, the Arboretum, University of Guelph; Carol Ann Lacroix, director, the Herbarium, the University of Guelph; R. D. Lawrence; Glen Lumis, professor, landscape horticulture, University of Guelph; Alan McNab; Zenia Miller; Andrea Mudry-Fawcett, manager, external communications, the University of Guelph; Wynn Newbery; Gordon Ridgley; Diane Rimstead; Mary Jane Rogers; Alan Watson, director, the Arboretum, University of Guelph; Shirley Whittington, information officer for Huronia Historical Parks.

The author and photographer thank the gardeners: Bill Bartels; Susan Biggar; Marie Bergsma; Helen Boggild; Elizabeth Bryce; Ann and Donald Campbell; David Campbell; Babs Carr; Aileen Coates; Jennifer Dattels; Kathy Dembroski; Maurice Desroches, agricultural artisan, Sainte-Marie Among the Hurons; Ted Donaldson, head gardener, Llanllar; Michael Edgecombe; Jill Farrow; Julia Foster; Jim French; Jeannie Guillet; Lynn Hancock; Peggy Harvey; Anne and Peter Hertzberg; Barbara Hill; Chris Hughes; Thomas Jarvis; Ron Jean-Marie and Carolyn Moore; Lorena Laferrière; R. D. Lawrence; Margo McGregor; Duggan Melhuish; Suzann Partridge; Virginia Peake; Timothy Regan; Frances Reid; Jeff and Linda Reid; Marion and Jim Robinson; Gilbert and Earlene Sutton; Caley Taylor; Jim Tait; George Woerner; Brenda Yates.

The author is indebted to Ray Timson for his cogent advice — Details, details!" and "Never assume anything" — and for joyfully taking on a greater share of childcare for two summers and to Harry Bartlett Timson for cheering up his mom. The author cherishes the examples of Reginald Bartlett Newbery, still growing a huge crop of vegetables in his tenth decade, the late Dorothy Prowse Newbery, who gardened first at her home on Tondern Island, and Wynn Newbery, who sets a high standard in gardening as in everything. Norman and Sue Newbery provided bed, breakfast and cheer en route to farflung gardens. For timely words of encouragement the author is grateful to Beland Honderich — "You must keep on with your writing," to Judith Timson — "A book would be perfect for you," and to Sylvia Cutmore — "All you need is an idea." Publisher John Denison, editors Noel Hudson and Kathleen Fraser, and designer Gillian Stead bring to their trade intensely honed skills, humour and civility.

In addition, the photographer wishes to thank the staff of the Colourchrome Laboratories for processing film for the project, Ted Knight and Kodak Canada for early samples of the latest Ektachrome transparency film, and Minolta Canada.

❧ BIBLIOGRAPHY ❧

Brown, D. M., G. A. McKay and L. J. Chapman. *The Climate of Southern Ontario.* Toronto: The Department of Transport, Canada, Meteorological Branch, 1968

Bryan, Ruby Gibbins and Muriel E. Newton-White. *Wildflowers of the North.* Cobalt: Highway Book Shop, 1978

Chapman, L. J. *The Physiography of Southern Ontario,* Second Edition. Toronto: University of Toronto Press, 1966

Coatsworth, David. *Farmers of the East: Huron Indians.* Toronto: Ginn and Co., 1975

Cody, William J. and Donald M. Britton. *Ferns and Fern Allies of Canada.* Ottawa: Agriculture Canada, 1989

Fitzgibbon, Agnes and C. P. Traill. *Canadian Wildflowers.* Montreal: John Lovell, 1868, republished Toronto: Coles Publishing Co., 1972

Hamelin, Louis-Edmond. *Canada: A Geographical Perspective.* Toronto: Wiley Publishers of Canada Ltd., 1973

Johnson, Lorraine. *The Ontario Naturalized Garden.* Vancouver/Toronto: Whitecap Books, 1995

Lellinger, David B. *A Field Manual of the Ferns and Fern-Allies of the United States & Canada.* Washington: Smithsonian Institution Press, 1985

Lima, Patrick. *The Harrowsmith Perennial Garden.* Camden East: Camden House, 1989

Osler, Mirabel. *A Gentle Plea for Chaos.* New York: Simon and Schuster, 1989

Soper, James and Margaret Heimburger. *Shrubs of Ontario.* Toronto: Royal Ontario Museum, 1982

Trudel, Marcel. *The Beginnings of New France 1524-1663.* Toronto: McClelland and Stewart Ltd., 1973

Whitner, Jan Kowalczewski. *Stonescaping.* Pownal, NY: Garden Way Publishing, 1992

Wright, J. V. *Ontario Prehistory.* Ottawa: National Museums of Canada, 1972

Wright, Ronald. *Stolen Continents.* Toronto: Viking, 1992

Zichmanis, Zile and James Hodgins. *Flowers of the Wild Ontario and the Great Lakes Region.* Toronto: Oxford University Press, 1992

❦ RESOURCES ❦

CANADIAN WILDFLOWER SOCIETY
Unit 12A, Suite 228,
4981 Highway 7E.,
Markham, Ont.
L3R 1N1
(905) 294-9075
Membership includes seed exchange, plant sources, magazine.
Free brochure.

THE GARDEN CLUB OF TORONTO
777 Lawrence Ave. E.
Don Mills, Ont.
M3C 1P2
(416) 447-5218

GOSLING WILDLIFE GARDEN
The Arboretum
University of Guelph
Guelph, Ont.
N1G 2W1
(519) 824-4120 ext. 2113
fax: (519) 763-9598
Plant collections show how to increase diversity of backyard habitats
and attract wildlife. Open daily.

HUNTSVILLE HORTICULTURAL SOCIETY
Dates and map for annual garden tour available from:
Huntsville and Lake of Bays Chamber of Commerce
8 West St. N., Box 1470
Huntsville, Ont.
P1H 2B6
(705) 789-4771

MUSKOKA HERITAGE FOUNDATION
Box 482
Bracebridge, Ont.
P1L lP8
Heritage resource centre, "green" store, 9 Taylor Rd., Bracebridge
(705) 645-7393

SAINTE-MARIE AMONG THE HURONS
Huronia Historical Parks
Box 160, Midland, Ont.
L4R 4K8
(705) 526-7838
Audio-visual presentation, reconstruction of seventeenth-century
palisaded mission, museum, candlelight tours. Season opens
Victoria Day weekend.

Species List
Technical Appendix of Natural Heritage Evaluation of Muskoka, June
1995, by R. L. Bowles, B. M. Bergsma and Ron Reid for the Muskoka
Heritage Areas Program of the District Municipality of Muskoka and
the Muskoka Heritage Foundation. This list of vascular plants,
mushrooms, breeding birds, herpetofauna, mammals, butterflies is
available for $10.70, including tax, at:
District Municipality of Muskoka
10 Pine St.
Bracebridge, Ont.
P1L 1N3